CHURCHILL, EISENHOWER, AND THE MAKING OF THE MODERN WORLD

Churchill, Eisenhower, and the Making of the Modern World

Christopher Catherwood

LYONS
PRESS

Essex, Connecticut

An imprint of Globe Pequot, the trade division of
The Rowman & Littlefield Publishing Group, Inc.
4501 Forbes Blvd., Ste. 200
Lanham, MD 20706
www.rowman.com

Distributed by NATIONAL BOOK NETWORK

Copyright © 2023 by Christopher Catherwood

British Library Cataloguing in Publication Information available

Library of Congress Cataloging-in-Publication Data
Names: Catherwood, Christopher, author.
Title: Churchill, Eisenhower, and the making of the modern world /
    Christopher Catherwood.
Description: Essex, Connecticut : Lyons Press, [2023] | Includes
    bibliographical references and index. | Summary: "Explores how two great
    WWII leaders, Winston Churchill and Dwight Eisenhower, created the
    postwar world order that lasted for nearly seventy-five years"—
    Provided by publisher.
Identifiers: LCCN 2022014728 (print) | LCCN 2022014729 (ebook) | ISBN
    9781493050529 (hardcover) | ISBN 9781493050536 (epub)
Subjects: LCSH: World politics—1945–1989. | Churchill, Winston, 1874–1965.
    | Roosevelt, Franklin D. (Franklin Delano), 1882-1945. | United
    States—Foreign relations—Great Britain. | Great Britain—Foreign
    relations—United States. | Democratization—History—20th century. |
    World War, 1939–1945—Diplomatic history. | Cold War.
Classification: LCC D843 .C338 2023 (print) | LCC D843 (ebook) | DDC
    909.82—dc23/eng/20220401
LC record available at https://lccn.loc.gov/2022014728
LC ebook record available at https://lccn.loc.gov/2022014729

In loving memory of my beloved wife, Paulette, (1952–2018), my relationship with whom embodied the "special relationship"

And good friend Jonathan Sandys (1975–2018), Winston Churchill's great-grandson and advocate in the United States for his ancestor's true greatness

And two friends and colleagues for over a quarter of a century, whose INSTEP Study Abroad Programme in Cambridge, England, gave many American students a taste of British life: Professor Geoffrey Williams (1930–2020) and his wife, Janice Williams (1945–2021)

Contents

ACKNOWLEDGMENTS

THIS IS THE FIRST BOOK THAT HAS BEEN ALMOST ENTIRELY WRITTEN after the death of my wife, Paulette, in 2018. She and I embodied a "special relationship" of our own: I am British and Paulette was American, more specifically a Virginian. Ours was one of many years of wedded happiness, and so it was a "special relationship" of considerable success. She knew this book would be happening, and it is sad that she never lived long enough to see it in print.

My former literary agent, Eugene Brissie, enabled this book to happen when he became a co–editorial director at Lyons Press. He therefore deserves double gratitude, as do two literary friends in Britain, Andrew Hayward, formerly my publisher here in Britain and still a pillar of support, and Richard Reynolds, of Heffers bookshop in Cambridge, and the doyen of many literary prizes and awards. They kept the flame of this book alive during Paulette's final years. Thanks also to production editor Meredith Dias and copy editor Ann Seifert.

My mother, Elizabeth Catherwood, survived the blitz! She was evacuated from London only to return there in time for the V1 and V2 rockets to start hitting the capital. Aged ninety-three, she is happily very much with us still. In recent months my mother and I have been together in lockdown and my gratitude and warmth for my mother is as strong now as it was when I came into the world over sixty years ago. The generation that endured the war is unique and my mother is its embodiment.

Sadly no longer alive is Geoffrey Williams, whom I have succeeded as the Academic Director of the Wake Forest INSTEP programme here in Cambridge. He also survived the blitz, the V1 and the V2 and went on to become a successful professor embodying the "special relationship" in his decades of leadership of the INSTEP programme, in which American students from Wake Forest, Villanova, Tulane, Spelman, and other excellent academic institutions in the United States would come and spend a term in Cambridge, very ably assisted administratively by his wife Janice, who died in 2021. He retired at the age of eighty-seven, which is an inspiration to us all! His insights and cheerfulness, and that of his wife, are missed on both sides of the Atlantic. Steve Seaworth and Doreen Woolfrey have been stalwarts of INSTEP for many years and happily stayed with the program when it transferred to Wake Forest. And a list of students whom I have had the joy of teaching over the past quarter century would be too long to print!

The final dedicatee of this book is Jonathan Sandys, a great-grandson of Winston Churchill, who tragically died while still in his forties not so long ago. His own life symbolized the "special relationship" in that he moved happily to Houston in Texas, where he married an American, and his children therefore are both descendants of Churchill and US citizens, in their case by birth. Jonathan's enthusiasm will be enormously missed by the many who knew him on both sides of the Atlantic. Getting to know many of his immediate family, including his mother and sister, has been wonderful, especially having a strong commitment to Christian faith very much in common.

Most of my works on Churchill have been written in their entirety at the glorious Churchill Archives Centre at Churchill College Cambridge. I have had the joy of being associated with this institution since 2004, more formally in recent years by being an Associate of their Senior Combination Room and for two separate semesters an Archives By-Fellow of the College. For anyone interested in Churchill, the archives are sheer bliss, and they have been magnificently run for many years now by Allen Packwood, who was awarded the rank of Officer of the Order of the British Empire for his internationally acclaimed work.

He runs a very efficient and exceptionally happy team. Of the long-term staff, Andrew Riley (the archivist for the Thatcher Papers, that are also there) and his wife, Fiona, have become good friends, with Fiona being an inspiration to many in living so joyfully in spite of adverse health—in my wife's last years both Andrew and Fiona were fabulous for morale. The chairman of the Archives Committee, Dr. Adrian Crisp, is not only the most congenial of lunch companions, but also a renaissance man in that he is a senior medical practitioner, a historian, and a novelist and raconteur all rolled into one.

Churchill is also a most sociable place. The Master, Dame Athene Donald, and her husband, Matthew, run a college that is not just known globally for its academic excellence, but also a convivial community, for which the word *civilized* is surely apt. They and the now former Senior Tutor, Richard Partington, showed what collegiality was all about in terms of empathy when my wife died. Conversation at lunch is always fun, especially the way in which the distinguished astronomers take time to explain the complexities of cosmology to a mere historian. I could thank dozens of people, but here will name those who have come to mind as I write this: Professors Alec Boksenberg, Douglas Gough, Ray Goldstein, Mike Gregory, and Christopher Tout and the keeper of the Churchill art collection, Barry Phipps. The college computer specialist Jake Huggins embodies patience in dealing with technologically challenged colleagues.

My dinner at Churchill with Professor Mark Holmes, and visitors Dr. Daniel Larsen and Professor Noah Rogoff, at a time when my wife was dying, will long live in the memory both as a wonderful occasion— High Table discussion at its best and most enjoyable—and an event that even though brief was able to take my mind off my imminent widower status and realize that when she died I would not be without the kind of conversation that so embodied my marriage to her.

Dan Larsen is a distinguished historian at Trinity College Cambridge, and I must thank both him and former Trinity student Nathania Williams for their kindness and intellectual encouragement.

The Archives By-Fellowship brings many writers and historians to the college. Two of them have been of inestimable help in writing this book, and getting to know them has been a privilege and pleasure combined. My friend Graham Farmelo has, like me, had the honor of two by-fellowships, and we shared a desk while he was writing his book on Churchill and the bomb. Graham was awarded significant literary prizes for an earlier work during his time at the Archives, and he is now the official biographer of Stephen Hawking, a distinction fully deserved. Kevin Ruane, a fellow professional historian, has also written a work on Churchill and nuclear weapons, and it has been great to get to know the person whose books I have read with such profit. As ever, while I agree utterly with their writing, the conclusions in this book are my own.

Owing to COVID-19 restrictions, much of this book had to be written at the University Library in Cambridge, in their architecturally famous Main Reading Room. The staff has been help and kindness personified in these strange times, keeping the place open and ensuring that we can all work there safely. Sadly I do not know all their names—and most of them have been wearing masks—but they have done a superb job in most difficult circumstances. The Bracken Library of Churchill has come to the rescue on many occasions.

Friends made at university have, in my case and in Paulette's, turned out to be friends for life. For me Andrew and Clare Whittaker (and their daughters Charlotte and Rosie), and Andrew Kearsley and his wife Jonquil Drinkwater (and their child Jack and her parents Geoffrey and Gill Drinkwater) really have been friends for decades through thick and thin. My devotion and gratitude to all of them is beyond words. The same applies to friends of my wife's: Lamar and Betsy Weaver Brandt, Al and Elaine LaCour, Mike and Lucy Wilkins, Claude and Leigh Marshall (and their daughters Lauren, Emily, and Catherine—and now grandchildren as well), and Larry and Beth Adams have all become good and faithful friends of mine as well.

My church also embodies the success of the "special relationship": The Rector of All Saints Little Shelford, Simon Scott, is, like Churchill, an old Harrovian and English, and his wife Susu is an American from Pittsburgh. They have become dear friends through many hard times, and Simon was present in the hospital when Paulette died. All Saints is all that a church should be. The former curate Christopher Henderson and his wife Rachel were equally stalwart in Paulette's last days, as were people in the congregation too numerous to mention but who have all shown in countless ways what Christian support and kindness ought to be as has the new curate Edward Keene. Mark Smith, now Dean of Clare College Chapel, has been a tower of help as has also been the case with Alasdair Paine, Vicar of St Andrew the Great, and his wife Rachel (a fellow musician of my wife's), and their daughters Lucy and Alice. Thanks too to Professor Hill Gaston and his wife Chris for all their kindness and hospitality.

My gratitude to Nathan Buttery, now Vicar of All Saints Preston, and his wife Debbie and their family, is truly lifelong—they were there when

Paulette and I needed them and they have remained a rock of friendship since then.

Fellow historians have been a source of continuing inspiration. Richard Toye (also a Churchill biographer), John Treadway (and his wife Marina), and the writer Hugh Bicheno show what good history should be. None of them are responsible for anything I say in this book! Although not a historian, Professor Alexander McCall Smith's works kept my wife going in hospital, and my morale up since then. Knowing all of them and experiencing their encouragement and kindness has been a privilege.

My mother's caregivers, Irene Percifull and Demi Starling, have enabled me to leave my mother in safe hands while I have been working on this book. They and other people who help out looking after my mother embody what caregivers ought to be—people for whom it is a genuine vocation. Paulette's friend and former pupil Diana Edwards wonderfully arranged for my house to be tenanted while I was with my mother during COVID, and as the rental has been my main source of income for much of this period, Diana and my tenant Dr. Elizabeth Hampson in effect enabled me financially to finish this book.

My mother's friendship support group—"the Committee"—has been meeting most Tuesdays for over thirty years. Scilla Harvey (and her husband John), Pat Blake, and Margaret Macfarlane have become not just support for her, but in these strange times, for me as well.

I am very grateful to my friend Rev. Christopher Ash for giving a personal introduction to his brother Professor Timothy Garton Ash. Both brothers are internationally acclaimed authors, and for those of us who both know and love Central Europe, Professor Garton Ash's many books were essential reading during the exciting period of the fall of the Iron Curtain, to which he himself was a witness. I have been enjoying his work since he was present at the creation of Solidarity in Poland in 1980. His permission to quote from his two famous articles is much appreciated and not taken for granted. As always, though, the interpretations in this book are mine, and he is not responsible for them.

Introduction

ONE OF THE GREAT JOYS OF WRITING THIS BOOK WAS THE PRIVILEGE OF reading the correspondence between two of the giants of the twentieth century: Winston Churchill and Dwight D. Eisenhower. The Roosevelt-Churchill correspondence is well known and often cited, and now we have the chance to read in translation the letters between Churchill, Stalin, and Roosevelt during the Second World War. But the Eisenhower-Churchill missives are less well known, which is a shame because they are fascinating, not just as a historical record but also as insights into the minds of two people who helped shape the world in which we live today.

By late 1954 many of Churchill's colleagues were hoping that he would retire—he turned eighty on November 30 that year—and Eisenhower was sympathetic to those in Britain who felt Churchill should go out with a wonderful swan song and pass the torch to others. So on July 22 he wrote an unusually long missive to the prime minister, most of which was on matters of urgency, but some of which was reflective: What could Churchill do as a magnificent gesture of retirement?

As Eisenhower put it:

> *I am certain that you must have a very deep and understandable desire to do something special and additional to your remaining period of active service that will be forever recognized as a mile-stone in the world's tortuous progress toward a just and lasting peace. Nothing else could provide such a fitting climax to your long and brilliant service to your sovereign, your country and the world.*

Eisenhower was very aware that the Soviets were exploiting nationalism—in the 1950s the understandable desire of colonized peoples to be free of foreign imperial rule. This disturbed him, and therefore an idea came to him as he wrote. He suggested to Churchill that the prime minister make "a thoughtful speech on the subject of the rights to self-government."

He did not forget that Britain was still very much a colonial power. So he reiterated that in his recent discussions with Churchill, "we agreed that in a number of areas peoples are not yet ready for self-rule" and any attempts to speed the process "would be to condemn them to lowered standards of life and possibly to communistic domination." But self-rule was nonetheless vital. "Colonialism is on the way out as a relationship among peoples. The sole question is one of aim and method. I think we should handle it so as to win adherents to Western aims." And getting newly freed nations on the side of the West would thwart the machinations of the Kremlin.

As Eisenhower put it:

> *To make use of the spirit of nationalism, we must show for it a genuine sympathy; we must prove that the obstacles that now prevent self-government to certain regions genuinely concern the free world and engage our earnest purpose to work for their elimination.*

And Churchill, so far as Eisenhower was concerned, was an ideal person to begin the process upon which the president now wished the free West to embark. He began with education: "A speech on this matter—and no other could so well do it as you—should deal with the need." Ideally there would be a time frame in which all these goals could be achieved. He then told Churchill:

> *If you could then say that twenty-five years from now, every last one of the colonies (excepting military bases) should have been offered a right to self-government and determination [underlined in original] you would electrify the world.*

Toward the end of his epistle (which he sent by mail rather than telegram so that only Churchill himself could see it), he added:

I long to find a theme which is dynamic and gripping and which our two countries can espouse together. In this way, we can exercise the world leadership to which the communists aspire. Also by working together for concrete constructive goals, we can cement our relationship in a way that is only possible if there is fellowship in deeds. We found that fellowship in war, and we must equally try to find it in peace. . . . Therefore, I bespeak [sic] your cooperation and indeed your initiative in opening what could be a great new chapter in history.

Today we would applaud such sentiments from the rooftops. Eisenhower had understood that the wishes of colonial peoples for independence were legitimate, and his vision of the unity of free peoples was surely an exciting one.

On August 8, 1954, Churchill replied:

I read with great interest all that you have written to me about what is called colonialism, namely: bringing forward backward races and opening up the jungles. I was brought up to feel very proud of much that we have done. Certainly in India, with all its history, religion and ancient forms of despotic rule, Britain has a story to tell which will look quite well against the background of the coming hundred years.

Backward races and opening up jungles! But he had to confess: "As a matter of fact the sentiments and ideas which your letter expressed are in full accord with the policy now being pursued in all the Colonies of the British Empire."

Here he was correct—three years later Malaya, with all its jungles, gained its independence, and so too did the Gold Coast (now known as Ghana), the first African state to gain its freedom.

But Churchill had a confession to make to Eisenhower:

In this I admit I am a laggard. I am a bit sceptical about universal suffrage for the Hottentots even if refined by proportional representation. The British and American Democracies were slowly and painfully forged and even they are not perfect yet.

Eisenhower wanted his old friend to have a "swan song" theme, and rather than the end of colonialism, Churchill chose his great refrain: "I think I will stick to the old one, 'The Unity of the English-speaking peoples.' With that all will work out well."

The truths, as the US Constitution says, are self-evident. The gulf between the worldviews of the two correspondents is clear for all to see. Yet the two men worked together for fourteen years, from 1941 to 1955, and an enormous degree of warmth grew between them despite their differences. There was mutual respect, even if, on Eisenhower's side, it sometimes turned into exasperation or incredulity. But it worked. And between them they helped create in the 1950s an era in which the kind of war in which they fought side by side in the 1940s became unthinkable.

Chronologically this book needs to begin with the Second World War, with Eisenhower the unknown young staff officer and Churchill the political leader of the great British Empire.

World War II must be one of the most written about events in history—surely the best-known and most thoroughly analyzed six years that have ever taken place. Every battle or campaign has its anniversaries, and new books pore over each minute detail, now more difficult to obtain as the last veterans pass into memory. Yet new facts emerge, as well as new perspectives and new arguments over long-fought battles of interpretation.

Hindsight, according to US baseball legend Yogi Berra, is always 20/20. What is obvious to us in retrospect, nearly (at time of writing) eighty years after the war ended, is often far from the case to those who were there at the time.

The revelation of Ultra—the code breakers of Bletchley Park and similar achievements with Japanese codes in the United States—meant that dozens of hitherto authoritative books published in the 1950s and 1960s had to be rewritten, now that we know the Allied generals had full details of enemy preparations in as close to real time as was then feasible.

Similarly, the brief period in which nearly all the Soviet archives were opened has completely changed the way in which we examine the war on the Eastern Front, where over four-fifths of German troops engaged in a war of horror not seen since Genghis Khan or Tamerlane. And no longer do we see Stalin in the benign "Uncle Joe" perspective that the Western Allies perceived him during the war. We no longer forget the price paid by Poland and other nations during the period of the Molotov-Ribbentrop Pact of 1939–1941, or the fact that for many Europeans foreign occupation and tyranny did not end in 1945 but continued to 1989 or 1991.

Decisions made during the war have created the world in which we live today. We are still living with the consequences, and the current map of Europe was drawn up based on the decisions of the victorious Allies.

In addition, the war confirmed the United States as the number-one world power. It may now hold that position tenuously with the rise of China, but at the time of writing, the power and global reach of the United States remained unique in its strength. This change effectively took place during the Second World War, and the power structure created at its end still exists—the five victorious nations in 1945 are the permanent members of the United Nations Security Council to this day, with only Britain's place (post-Brexit) *possibly* up for discussion and then only if the country breaks up in the event of Scottish independence.

So for all intents and purposes, we live in the world that emerged from the rubble of World War Two. The only subsequent massive change could be said to be the disintegration of the Soviet bloc in 1989 in Central/Eastern Europe, with the consequent reunification of Germany and freedom for the former "satellite states," followed in 1991 by the breakup of the USSR (Union of Soviet Socialist Republics) itself into many different countries, leaving a still powerful but deeply reduced Russian state, no longer a match for the might of the West. There are now NATO troops in the Baltic states not far from St. Petersburg (and the fact that the city is no longer called Leningrad or even Petrograd in itself speaks volumes).

But in 1942, when we start our story, the world to which we have become so accustomed today was unthinkable and unforeseeable. In early 1942, Hitler, his progress stopped at Moscow in December 1941, was still in a powerful military position with his armies in the USSR, and the crucial naval base of Singapore had fallen to the mighty Japanese onslaught.

In 1942 the decisions that had to be made were by definition short-term—what needed to be done immediately—so that the new allies, the

United Kingdom and the United States, could stem the tide toward a German-Japanese victory (not forgetting the much less powerful Axis nations such as Italy and Romania). That is what mattered, and the long-term decisions, those that created the world in which we live today, were unfathomable. A world in which German and Japanese militarism would be permanently halted, in which there would be two superpowers, the United States and USSR, and a drastically reduced British Empire in which India would be independent at last—none of these scenarios were even remotely conceivable or on the near horizon. Just over three years later, in 1945, the beginnings of an entirely unpredictable new world order would emerge, but the decisions made in 1942 were solely about keeping the war going.

The argument of this book is that many of the decisions that created the modern world happened by mistake or, rather, without thought of their longer-term consequences. The world created in 1945 existed because of decisions made in the heat of war, *at that time* before Allied victory seemed inevitable. The tyranny of the urgent prevailed, and it is only now, decades later, that we can see what they could not. And since Eisenhower was there with Churchill at the beginning in 1941, and again in an utterly changed relationship in 1955, I have looked at them in particular in order to tell this tale.

Personal events have made what you are reading different because the context in which I am writing them now was radically altered from when the idea first began to germinate in discussions some years ago in the Churchill Senior Combination Room. (The main change for your author is that my wife was alive at the beginning and died before I contacted Eugene Brissie to see if this was a viable project.) When the contract was signed, Donald Trump was president of the United States, and without in any way being politically partisan—your author is British—the way in which the transatlantic was seen was a radical departure from the postwar world order created in 1945 to 1949—from the Yalta Conference of 1945 to the creation of NATO in 1949. As I am writing this, Joe Biden has become president, and the transatlantic order that existed from 1949 to 2017 shows every sign of being restored, albeit in a new context with China now being the rival hegemon to the United States in place of the USSR (1945–1991). But in 2024 that could change all over again.

And the time in which this chapter is written, the British prime minister, Boris Johnson, a very considerable fan of Winston Churchill (and author of the bestselling *The Churchill Factor*), has leaked through aides and journalists that he sees the term "special relationship," the iconic phrase of Winston Churchill, as revealing something "needy and weak." The powerful closeness of the US/UK link still continues, of course, and President Biden has affirmed it, but it is a major change in perception for a *British* prime minister to say such a thing, even unofficially. Whether or not he is right will be examined in the conclusion to this book, but all these things are worth bearing in mind. And all this could change overnight; such are the exigencies of modern politics.

New developments that alter our view of the past with major shifts in perspective are continually emerging: A book written in 1988, before the fall of the Iron Curtain, by definition does not see what a book written in 1992 can understand much better, and now, thirty years since the fall of the USSR, it's clear that much of the excitement and optimism of 1989 to 1991 was tragically misplaced.

But the key factor in the making of the modern world, and of the story of the "special relationship" or whatever we now call it, is that by 1945, by Yalta, by Postdam, by the initial discussions in San Francisco that led to the United Nations, all these events were conditioned by the result of decisions made earlier.

And by the time Churchill became prime minister again in 1951 and Eisenhower was first elected president in 1952, the results of those decisions had created a whole new world: one that had an Iron Curtain dividing Europe, and a NATO alliance designed to keep the USSR behind that line, one that involved an entire American army, air force, and navy based in Europe—*in peacetime*. Eisenhower, who in 1945 refused to sacrifice American lives to capture Berlin, was by 1952 someone who detested the Soviet Union and its policies. And of course the atomic bomb, designed to prevent the loss of the lives of hundreds of thousands of US servicemen in a land invasion of Japan, utterly changed the world forever, as Churchill came to realize.

If in the Second World War Eisenhower was more of a dove and Churchill the hawk, it could be argued that in the 1950s those roles were reversed. But so too was the power relationship between the two men, in a way that was inconceivable when Eisenhower made his first trip to London in 1942.

This arguably is what makes history exciting—who in 1988 would have predicted the fall of the Iron Curtain, or in 2000 would have foreseen 9/11 and its many consequences? No expert on British politics would, during the Munich crisis of late 1938, ever have predicted that in May 1940 Winston Churchill would be prime minister. In 1942 no one had heard of Dwight Eisenhower, yet in 1944 he was the Supreme Allied Commander for D-Day, an accomplishment that would see him win the presidency of his country in 1952. Even in the dark days of 1940, Britain could, especially with Churchill in office, persuade itself that Britannia ruled the waves. By the 1950s the balance of power between the United Kingdom and its former colony, the United States, had irrevocably altered, as Churchill came to discover.

How then did these two people create the modern world? What happened to the special tie with the United States that Churchill so valued? And never forget, we know their future, but they did not.

⁃ ⁓

Just after the original manuscript of this book was sent to the publisher, news from Ukraine seemed to be bad, but not of the kind likely to launch a war. Then, at the proof stage, war erupted, and is continuing at the current time of writing. The heroic resistance of the Ukrainian people has brought the complete solidarity of most in the West, with the United Kingdom being at the vanguard of military aid. And as ours is a book about Winston Churchill, the Ukrainian President Volodymyr Zelensky and his bravery and rhetoric have brought many Churchillian parallels to mind among British audiences and in the United States as well.

Thankfully the ideals of the postwar settlement of 1945 and the creation of NATO in 1949 have sprung again to life, with the West gloriously united in its moral support for the Ukrainian cause. The values so cherished by both Churchill and Eisenhower are at the center of that solidarity of purpose.

As of this moment the future of the war remains uncertain, but Churchill and Eisenhower would surely have been proud of the response to the greatest European military crisis since the Second World War.

1

Deciding the Course of the War

WHEN WERE THE KEY DECISIONS MADE THAT DECIDED BOTH THE COURSE of the war and its outcome? People often think they know, but there is a good case for stating that the traditional narrative is in fact mistaken. It is this idea—that perceptions may not be wholly accurate—that we will pursue in the next few chapters, with the results we will see later in this book, including how developments in World War II and later in the Cold War defined the evolution of the modern world and in particular what Winston Churchill was to call the "special relationship" or, from the title of one of his books on the conflict, the "grand alliance." This chapter will cast a glance at events in 1942 and 1943, some very familiar and others perhaps skated over but of long-term importance nonetheless. This is not a new history, with revelations unfamiliar to specialists, but it is perhaps for many a different way of looking at the past. And in all this, Eisenhower made a key difference even before he appeared in London in person.

And in recent years there is also a new way of thinking, which contends that two events took place in *December 1941* (the title of Evan Mawdsley's book) that, in effect, sealed *eventual* Allied victory: the entry of the United States into the war and the German failure to capture Moscow. While the war would have over three years to go (May 1945 in Europe and August 1945 in the Pacific), the combination of American entry and Soviet survival meant that there was no longer any realistic way in which the Third Reich and the Japanese Empire could possibly hope to win. It was now a *world* war on a terrifying and global scale.

That is not to say the Allies would not have terrible losses. Not long after Churchill's return from his trip to Washington, DC, in December 1941, the British lost the vital naval base of Singapore to the Japanese. Many battles would be waged on the Eastern Front between Germany and the USSR, in which millions of soldiers would die (estimates vary but perhaps as many as *twelve million* Soviet troops would die by the end of the war). The inevitability of Allied victory might, we would now consider, have been evident in December 1941, but *at that time* there was no possible way the Allies could foresee that, however obvious it seems to us in retrospect.

So when British-American talks began in Washington, DC, in 1941 and then transferred to Britain in early 1942, neither country was remotely taking anything for granted. And for the United Kingdom, much indeed looked dire. Churchill was right to believe in the United States, but by no means did everyone share that point of view.

For many who write about the war and its aftermath, the new world was born at Yalta in 1945 or perhaps slightly earlier at Tehran in 1943, when Churchill, Roosevelt, and Stalin met for the first time in person.

But there is a good case for saying that it was the decisions made in 1942 and earlier in 1943, before Tehran, that in reality made all the difference. And these were decisions in which Eisenhower, then an ordinary officer, played a vital part, from his arrival in the United Kingdom in 1942, becoming an Allied commander later that year and Supreme Allied Commander in 1944 for D-Day, then crucially becoming NATO's first military boss in 1950 and president of the United States in 1953. Only he had that unique degree of continuity with Churchill from 1941 to 1955 in terms of key figures from the United States and the United Kingdom, and that is why a biographical parallel between the two men is the means used in this book to narrate how our modern world was created.

The reason why discussions in Washington, DC, in December 1941, in which Eisenhower was only a distant observer, and those in 1942, in some of which he was a key player, ended up altering entirely how the Second World War would end, shall be examined later in this chapter. But first we need to find out how Eisenhower's brilliant planning—upon which Roosevelt and Marshall signed off—was received by the British, before we go on to consider the consequences.

Eisenhower's biographer, Stephen Ambrose, in his book *Eisenhower and Berlin 1945*, an entire volume on just one of the Supreme Allied Commander's numerous wartime decisions, noted:

> *In 1942, when the British were making the largest contribution to the alliance and the [British and American] Combined Chiefs of Staff reached a deadlock, the British were able to insist upon their view and the alliance committed its strength to the Mediterranean. In late 1943, when the two nations were making a fairly equal contribution*

and the Combined Chiefs of Staff reached a deadlock, it took a third party—Stalin—to break it, and the alliance committed its strength to OVERLORD. In 1945, when the Americans were making the largest contribution and there was deadlock, the Americans insisted on their view and it was carried out.

In fact, this pertained only to those areas of the conflict in which the British and Americans were the key players. The bulk of World War II was fought not in North-West Europe but on the Eastern Front—which of course is why Stalin was able to intervene in the way that he did. And in the conflict in the Pacific, outside of the Indo-Burmese front, the US Navy carried out the overwhelming amount of the fighting. As Ambrose points out in the same book, by 1945, "the British contribution to Allied resources was down to 25 percent of the whole."

That was 1945, when there were some five million British troops under arms, and eleven million American troops—over twice the number. And that is to ignore the Soviets, the creators of the Red Army, perhaps the biggest military force ever assembled in history.

But in April 1942, the decision (made in April 1945) whether the Western Allies or the Soviets should take Berlin was three years into the future. And although Churchill's dream that the United States would enter the war on the British side had come gloriously true in December 1941, as of the discussions between the US delegation to Britain and the British, there were no Allied forces in Europe, and the United Kingdom had just suffered the loss of Singapore to the Japanese, as well as serious setbacks against the Germans in Greece and North Africa the previous year. So what the Americans with their can-do spirit thought should easily be possible, and what the British, with a recent history of humiliation and retreat, thought *might* just be possible, were two very different things.

And long-term memories were seared into the British consciousness as well, as becomes rapidly apparent.

Today we know that D-Day—the issue the Americans had crossed the Atlantic to discuss with their new British allies—was a success. But in 1942, to predict that the Americans—especially future great military geniuses such as Eisenhower—would be vindicated could not be taken for granted. Even in 1942 the United States was the mightiest economy on earth. But the 1930s had been spent in isolation, and Churchill had been one of a derided minority when he sang its praises during his years in the political wilderness. One could say that the Americans *at this moment* were like a giant but with no more than a child's bow and arrow. This is the perspective that is the essential understanding to what unfolds in this chapter.

Eisenhower had put forward a plan on how the Allies could recapture North-West Europe and defeat Germany—though the plan carried the name of his superior, the US Army Chief of Staff, General George C. Marshall, who headed the US delegation along with President Roosevelt's spokesman, Harry Hopkins. When we read the debate that followed, we forget a vital piece of hindsight: We know the death toll for D-Day in 1944 compared to the carnage on the first day of the Somme, July 1, 1916. Some 4,000 Allied soldiers died on the beaches of Normandy, 1,400 of whom were British or Canadian. By contrast 19,000 British soldiers died on the fateful opening day in 1916, or thirteen times as many deaths as occurred on June 6, 1944. If one includes those injured, the toll for the opening of the Somme Offensive reaches 57,000, which is the highest casualty rate for any British engagement.

The horror of that day and of other days like it in the First World War stuck permanently with those who survived. And the young officers of that war were the generals of the Second World War. Never again would July 1, 1916, be repeated.

And so, correctly and inevitably, the British politicians and commanders who now carried the burden of decision-making were doing so under the shadow of the Somme. Lives mattered. Germany had to be beaten but not at the cost of the loss of life in the trenches in Flanders. When questioned by General George C. Marshall's official biographer, Forrest Pogue, Churchill's personal Chief of Staff, General Sir Hastings "Pug" Ismay could not emphasize this enough, as we shall see. The ghost of the carnage lived on—and understandably so.

So the planning for the liberation of Europe, what we now call D-Day, strongly reflected this. Thankfully for those landing on the Normandy beaches on June 6, 1944, Eisenhower was no Field Marshal Haig, and Montgomery was no General Rawlinson. The Allied troops landing in France were well prepared, ably led, and commanded by veterans who had learned the lessons of the earlier conflict. And alongside Commonwealth forces from Britain and Canada were America's finest, the Greatest Generation. Twenty-five hundred Americans were killed on D-Day, just over an eighth of the British casualties twenty-eight years earlier.

What America promised, it delivered. Fewer British and American soldiers died throughout the entire Second World War than Allied troops were killed, maimed, or injured in the Battle of the Somme in 1916.

However, right up until D-Day itself, until the first wave of Allied troops had established their bridgehead, both Churchill and his Chief of Staff General Sir Alan Brooke, were convinced that there would be carnage on the beaches of Normandy, a first day of the Somme all over again.

As Winston Churchill told his wife, Clementine, in the Cabinet Office map room the night before, "Do you realize that by the time you wake up in the morning twenty thousand men may have been killed?"

Brooke, meanwhile, confided to his diary that same night:

It is very hard to believe that in a few hours the cross Channel invasion starts! I am very uneasy about the whole operation. At the best it will fall so very very short of the expectation of the bulk of people, namely all those who know nothing of its difficulties. At the worst it may well be the most ghastly disaster of the whole war. I wish to God it were safely over.

In Brooke's view Eisenhower, the Supreme Allied Commander, was a mere coordinator, certainly no strategist of the kind that the war needed. By May 1945 Eisenhower's strategic genius as the creator of victory in the West was obvious to everyone open-minded. How wrong Brooke and Churchill had been.

The Second World War has probably—indeed certainly—had more written about it than any other conflict in history, which is hardly surprising given that at least fifty million people died during its course. We still live in the world that it created, many decades later.

This is not yet another attempt to reinterpret the often highly divisive history of that gargantuan conflict. But as British Cold War/Eastern Europe specialist Timothy Garton Ash perceptively wrote as far back as 1987—while the Cold War still seemed to be everlasting even though it had only two more years to run—we cannot understand the decades *after* the war unless we have a clear grasp of some of the events *during* the war. When Churchill was prime minister in peacetime (1951–1955), overlapping Eisenhower as president of the United States (1953–1961), they were living in a world that existed as the direct result of decisions made in the early years of the Second World War, as well as those made toward the end of it.

Let us take an example. In 1945 Churchill wanted the West to capture Berlin for what were essentially political reasons, to deny it as a prize for Stalin. Eisenhower realized the casualty rate for its seizure would be exceedingly high; when the Soviets did capture the city in May 1945, it cost the Red Army as many casualties as all the American deaths in the entire war put together.

In defying Churchill, Eisenhower was strategically right. But why was the Red Army already so close to Berlin—something that made their fight for it far more logical? That was the result of *political* decisions made earlier in the war. Books written by the main historians of the Eastern Front in 2020 and 2021 remind us that even when the Germans were at the gates of Moscow in 1941, with the Soviet capital in imminent danger of collapse, Stalin was demanding of the British that the United Kingdom recognize the sordid Molotov-Ribbentrop Pact of August 1939 in which the USSR and the Third Reich carved up Central Europe between them and once again obliterated Poland from the map. (Again, Timothy Garton Ash, one of the world's experts on this region, also pointed this out back in 1987.) To the American military mind—General George C. Marshall, Chief of Staff of the US Army, and victorious commander Dwight Eisenhower, the soldiers fought the war and then the politicians decided the outcome. In 1942, the date of this chapter, Eisenhower was a soldier, and Churchill the iconic global statesman. In 1953, Eisenhower was the most powerful politician in the West as president of the United

States, and Churchill a frail but still enthusiastic titan, leading a country that was losing its empire and its position in world affairs.

This is not a rerun of old stories! Rather it enables us to see how the balance of power between the two men—Churchill and Eisenhower—changed over the years, and did so because the shift in strength between the United Kingdom and the United States inexorably altered. We start, therefore, with a conflict—over wartime strategy—between the two countries, which, in April 1942, was won by Churchill. Then slowly but surely, including at the key Tehran Conference of 1943 when Churchill, Stalin, and Roosevelt met in person, it became evident to a saddened Churchill that Britain was the distinctly junior partner of the Big Three (United Kingdom, United States, USSR). The Big Two (Stalin and Roosevelt) settled on a US-Soviet agreement that the decision to invade continental Europe would happen in 1944, whether Churchill wished for that or not. The symbol of that change was that America chose the invasion's Supreme Allied Commander, Dwight Eisenhower, who would go on to win the war in the West just eleven months after D-Day in June 1944.

2

The British and American Ways of War

MILITARY HISTORIANS LOOK AT BATTLES, WITH THE AMERICAN authority Carlo D'Este being the iconic writer on the subject for the Second World War. Books such as his are gripping reads, as they have an exciting narrative; many of the best authors in this genre give you the feeling that you are on the battlefield, with the smell of cordite. And in purely *military* description they are unsurpassed. But is it always that straightforward? *Political* historians, of whom I am using international writer and expert Timothy Garton Ash as an exemplar in this chapter, have to *also* study the context. (Timothy Garton Ash was a personal eyewitness to much of the history about which he has written, understanding both the global context as a specialist but also knowing the key players in Central Europe in 1989 to 1991, and what it was like to be on a Stasi file in East Germany when he was a student there in the 1970s.)

Strategic decisions in April and May 1942 had profound consequences, subjecting Poland to Soviet tyranny from 1944 to 1989, not to mention most of the rest of Central and Eastern Europe, and, Jewish Holocaust experts reckon, the deaths of hundreds of thousands of Jews who would otherwise have survived.

It should be said here that the leading contemporary biographer of Churchill, Andrew Roberts, both in his definitive book on Churchill, Roosevelt, Marshall, and Brooke, *Masters and Commanders*, published in 2008, and in his magnum opus, *Churchill: Walking with Destiny*, in 2018, argues that Churchill's strategic victory over Marshall in 1942 helped save the war. (And it is wonderful to see a British writer acknowledge Marshall as a genius! Roberts is a rare example of someone from the United Kingdom who gives full due credit to Marshall's stature, having taken the trouble of an in-depth and in-person visit to the Marshall Archives and celebrated Thanksgiving with his appreciative hosts.) So the main consensus—supported, for instance, by another British-born historian also now in the United States, the widely revered Professor Paul Kennedy at Yale—is that in what follows Churchill made the right calls.

But by the time that a suppliant Churchill came to see an about-to-be-inaugurated Eisenhower in 1953, the decisions made less than a decade earlier had had the profoundest of consequences, the Cold War and the division of Europe by the Iron Curtain very much among them.

It's evident that one of the major problems we all face is we tend to read history backward. When we later consider the atom bomb discussions in the 1950s, we do so knowing that World War III has not yet happened. And after 1989, the Soviet bloc disintegrated, followed by the breakup of the seemingly eternal USSR itself in 1991. The same is true of what happened during the Second World War. What seemed inevitable to us in hindsight, especially the rise of the forty-plus-year Cold War (no one agrees on a fixed starting date, as we shall see), was not foreseeable then. We must always remember how people saw things *at the time in question.*

One of these is what would happen to the Soviet Union, following the German invasion, Barbarossa, in June 1941.

Today, academic opinion and works by thoughtful non-university authors who have also delved deep into the archives are of essentially one mind. The several specialized and thorough books by David Stahel on just 1941 alone, from the launch of Barbarossa to the German failure to capture Moscow in December 1941, argue that the invasion was doomed from the very moment it began. It was *by definition* impossible for the Wehrmacht to win and conquer the USSR, because the Soviet Union was too large, because the Red Army had millions of replacement forces for their losses in a way that the Germans did not, and also because—a somewhat neglected but crucial fact—the Soviets only had to fight on one front as a result of the Soviet-Japanese neutrality agreement on April 13, 1941, a treaty that surely changed the outcome of the war.

Books for wider audiences, such as those by Sir Rodric Braithwaite on Moscow in 1941, by Laurence Rees on the war generally, and by Jonathan Dimbleby on Barbarossa, make the same point. The German invasion was never going to succeed. And in hindsight this is incredibly obvious. The invaders might have won the key battle of Kharkov in 1942, but they went on to lose the battle for Stalingrad in 1942–43, and with the debacle at Kursk in 1943, in which both sides suffered hideous losses, the initiative was firmly back with the Red Army, which proceeded to bulldoze its way to ultimate victory in Berlin in May 1945.

One key fact that superb films such as *Saving Private Ryan* or television series such as *Band of Brothers* lead us to totally forget: *85 percent of German casualties were on the Eastern Front in 1941 to 1945.* The importance of this statistic cannot be emphasized enough. It is perhaps *the* key statistic of the whole war against Germany. And it was something that Stalin and the Soviets most decidedly never forgot, including Russians in the present, eight decades later.

When the British and Americans met from April through July 1942 in a series of vital planning meetings in London, what is abundantly plain to us now, eighty years onward, was not at all clear then. In October 1941 the Germans had captured the important city of Kharkov. In May 1942 the Soviets, despite having nearly twice as many troops as the Germans, not only failed to recapture the city, but suffered casualties ten times greater than those of the defending Germans. By the end of 1942, Case Blue, the German counteroffensive, would fail to capture Stalingrad and the vital Soviet oil fields of Baku. But to anxious British and American soldiers and politicians, this was in the future; what was obvious at the moment was that the Red Army was not doing well, despite the failure of the Wehrmacht to capture Moscow the previous December.

This, therefore, is the often forgotten context of the meetings with George C. Marshall and Harry Hopkins for the Americans, who were using material put together for them by one of Marshall's most prominent and able aides, a youngish staff colonel named Dwight Eisenhower. While Eisenhower was not physically in the room for the talks that took place, he might as well have been, since the plan that Marshall presented to his British allies was very much Eisenhower's thoughtful planning, detailed analysis, and strategic acumen.

There is one important caveat on these talks, which, among the many historians who have studied them, few, except once again Andrew Roberts in his great work *Masters and Commanders*, have realized. What Marshall was now laying before the British, using Eisenhower's scheme, were *two* plans, one a contingency plan called Sledgehammer, if the Soviet Union either collapsed or looked more than likely to collapse at some stage in 1942, and the second a long-term plan for the Allied liberation of Europe, to be launched in France in April 1943, the buildup to be code-named Bolero and the invasion itself provisionally called Roundup, what we now know by its later name of Overlord.

But these, as Eisenhower and Marshall intended, were *two* plans, not one. Historians have frequently conflated the two, and argued against an early date for the invasion of Europe because an invasion *in 1942* would have by definition had to be fought by British and Canadian forces, because by that year nowhere near enough Americans would have landed in Britain to take part.

And of course this is correct, as evidenced by the British-Canadian debacle at Dieppe in August 1942, when a premature raid against Nazi-occupied Europe by elite forces ended in disaster.

But Sledgehammer was a contingency. The full-scale invasion was Roundup, only to take place when enough US forces had landed in the United Kingdom to make a full-scale British-American-Canadian landing possible *in 1943*. In fact, the US forces planned for that invasion numbered *more American soldiers than actually landed in Normandy in 1944*. Eisenhower envisaged a greater US contingent than the number that landed successfully in France in June 1944. Similarly, more landing ships were planned for 1943 than were used in June 1944.

And once again, hindsight is a wonderful thing. D-Day was *not* a repeat of the Battle of the Somme; in fact, as we see later, it was not even remotely close in terms of casualties. In retrospect, the American can-do attitude proved to be entirely correct, and the wisdom of Eisenhower and Marshall entirely vindicated. (Some parts of the fighting in Normandy came close to some of that in Flanders, but not D-Day itself.)

Of course for the British the only precedent they had was the carnage of 1914 to 1918, of which the horrors of the Somme were but an episode in a four-year-long tale of death right until the final Allied breakthrough in the summer of 1918—helped in no small way by the arrival of large numbers of American troops in 1917, the unity of Allied command under French leadership, and the invention of the tank, a technical breakthrough in which Winston Churchill, both as First Lord of the Admiralty and later as Minister of Munitions, had played a crucial supporting role.

The other important fact is that the British and Americans had completely different philosophies of fighting a war. This is vital in that

Churchill's own most famous ancestor, John Churchill, First Duke of Marlborough, embodied much of the British way of thinking, which was the *indirect approach*—Great Britain relied on continental allies to fight the ground war while the Royal Navy commanded the seas. Most of Marlborough's soldiers at his great victories were part of a European coalition against France, and by no means necessarily British, and the same was true for the great Duke of Wellington at Waterloo in 1815. Britannia certainly ruled the waves, but the number of British soldiers committed to fighting in continental Europe itself was comparatively small, certainly in comparison with its land-based allies.

In 1914 much of the British army was defending the empire, often as far away as India, so the original British Expeditionary Force sent to aid France when the First World War broke out was far smaller than the army of France. It was the fact that the war continued, and became mired in the trenches, that made the government realize for the first time that an enormous *land* army was necessary, and this effectively took two years to put together. Not until 1916 did the United Kingdom, in collaboration with troops from the Empire (Canada, Australia, New Zealand, and India), have a full-strength military force with which to fight the Germans—and we all know what happened when the first major engagement was launched: 57,000 casualties on the opening day of the Somme Offensive.

Also part of the British tradition was to fight on the periphery rather than against the primary enemy head on. Take Marlborough's Battle of Blenheim, which was fought far from the main enemy, France, in Bavarian territory in what was to become Germany. Similarly, Wellington spent several years attacking French forces, but in Spain and Portugal, not engaging directly in France until 1814.

In the First World War, Churchill kept to his convictions, helping organize what turned out to be the disastrous attempt to eliminate the Ottoman Empire by attacking the Gallipoli peninsula, the Dardanelles, in 1915—a defeat that Australians remember to this day because so many of their soldiers died. In the end it was the arrival of the Americans and a change of fortune on the Western Front, in Flanders, that enabled the great Allied breakthrough of 1918 and an end to the conflict. Called the *peripheral approach*, it was a doctrine held by Churchill and all his military advisers.

Historically it made sense. Great Britain is an island and depends on trade for its prosperity, so the possession of the world's most powerful navy was an obvious prerequisite. Ruling the sea was essential to its survival. In terms of population, the United Kingdom (as it became in 1801) was far smaller than that of a giant land-based country such as France, and so to have continental allies with large armies to fight such a foe made complete sense. For the British, their doctrine was thus a logical outcome of their circumstances.

So a request to make the British think differently was asking Churchill and his key military advisers to go against the grain of centuries of British belief and practice.

What is odd is that someone as understanding of the United States as Churchill never fully grasped the game-changing implications of America entering the war. Consider just one statistic: By 1945 no less than 45 percent of all armaments were made in the United States, and probably 50 percent of everything manufactured. The scale of American industry and production was unprecedented in history, although it should also be noted that Soviet output, from factories far beyond German reach, was also gargantuan, with the T-34 tank being perhaps the prime example. But in sum the United States was unique—how right Churchill was to describe it as the "arsenal of democracy."

That logistical fact had profound implications for how the war was fought, and, of course, for how it was won. Books such as *Engineers for Victory* by Yale professor Paul Kennedy may not have riveting titles, but they are of absolute importance for understanding the overwhelming advantage the Allies enjoyed when the United States entered the conflict. It really was logistics, *logistics*, LOGISTICS. Kennedy's book shows this most helpfully.

But did Churchill and the British Chiefs of Staff actually grasp the titanic implications of all this? The Israeli historian Tuvia Ben-Moshe, in his revisionist work *Churchill: Strategy and History*, is so right when he discusses Churchill and the Chiefs of Staff's initial meetings with the Americans, with the former having a "fundamental defect" in their plans.

The United States' entry into the war, a development of revolutionary proportions, did not engender a revolutionary change in the prime minister's basic strategic conceptions (nor, for that matter, in those of his military advisers). This was despite the United States' enormous industrial and military potential, whose speedy realization during the previous war was a harbinger of things to come. The proposals contained in Churchill's plan held fast to strategic ideas he and his military advisers had conceived at a time when Britain stood alone, and which were a consequence of that situation.

In essence, to the British way of fighting, American entry into the war failed to alter their traditional way of thinking, which today seems extraordinary.

Long-term planning for victory was not based on the advantages possessed by the strongest Allied power (the United States); instead, and as had previously been the case, it rested on the strengths—and, to a greater extent, the weaknesses—of British military power.

And one can legitimately argue that this position never changed, with the British obsession with the peripheral approach paramount in their minds right until the end of the war in Europe.

The US approach, by contrast, was quite different. In adapting the original Victory Plan into hard propositions, Eisenhower was thinking like an American: find the main enemy, and go straight for that enemy with full strength until victory is won.

This strategy has a hallowed tradition, dating back to the Civil War in the 1860s. The great cry of Union general Fitz Henry Warren when he declared "On to Richmond!" was the declaration that the northern forces would go all out to conquer the South and capture its capital, Richmond.

This was the *direct approach*, and it also remained at the core of American strategy throughout the war. In 1945 it was the approach that won, under the command of Dwight Eisenhower.

The point, of course, is that the Americans had both the manpower and the logistical/industrial strength to bring about their wishes. Not merely that, but as people in Britain (and other parts of Europe) often forget, from 1941 to 1945 the United States fought two massive wars in two oceans, in the Atlantic against the Third Reich and in the Pacific against the Japanese. The Americans were able to fight what is called a two-ocean war, both the Atlantic and the Pacific, a feat without parallel in history. And they succeeded all the way to victory in both spheres.

Britain had realized in the 1930s that the United Kingdom simply did not have the strength to fight simultaneously in the Pacific and in Europe—this was the military rationale for the disastrous appeasement policy of that time. In 1941 that nightmare was fulfilled, with the British Empire at war with both Germany and Japan.

But a two-ocean conflict was not an American problem. What Eisenhower predicted would come to pass, and with the United States, by 1945, the greatest power on earth. The direct approach had *worked* because it was the United States, not Britain, in command of the war.

Churchill had always been right—the United Kingdom could not possibly do it on its own. Only American intervention could turn the tide. But sadly, so wedded was he to British military tradition that when the United States altered the course of the conflict by fulfilling his dream, he failed to grasp the implications. There is simply no other way to put it. The peripheral approach now had no need to continue—the Americans were coming!

However, the situation in April 1942, with the rearmament of the United States and the effects of conscription still in the future, meant that the British way of war still prevailed. And with the United States, like Britain, a democracy, electoral politics would also prove decisive. By the end of 1943, the Americans were able to insist on their way of war prevailing. But in 1942, Roosevelt realized, for US troops to be in action in Europe *immediately*, the need for a slow buildup of forces in Britain was dangerous to the Germany-first decision he and others had made back in 1941, before Pearl Harbor and before US entry into the war. So when the siren call came from Churchill to invade not North-West Europe but North Africa instead—the Mediterranean-based peripheral strategy—he had a president willing to listen.

3

Marshall Lays Out Eisenhower's Stall

WHEN, IN APRIL 1942, MARSHALL AND ROOSEVELT'S TOP AIDE, HARRY Hopkins, came to London to visit Churchill and the British Chiefs of Staff, they were presenting not just a plan over which Eisenhower and his team had labored hard for months, but a whole different way of doing war from their hosts, as we saw in the last chapter. As we shall see eventually, *this* time the British won, not for military reasons but for *political ones*, through the decision of President Roosevelt to ignore his own military advisers, Marshall and Eisenhower chiefly among them, and, for reasons of domestic American politics, to follow Churchill's plan.

The arguments in London, however, now in April 1942, and then the discussions in Washington, DC, were ostensibly both military and strategic. But, of course, just as Roosevelt's decision that year was fundamentally political, so too was Churchill's—the defense of the United Kingdom and the preservation globally of the British Empire and the United Kingdom's resultant geopolitical requirements. That is the background for the discussions that now took place, which is, arguably, why Marshall and Eisenhower lost out in the *short-term*, as for them it really was both military and strategic, as it would be for both of them during the rest of the war, even (or perhaps especially when) Eisenhower found himself elevated from humble planner to Supreme Allied Commander in 1942 to 1945.

As the last chapter showed, America's policy was simple—hit the main enemy first and head-on. And the point is this: *The United States was a big and powerful enough country and had a strong enough economy to do this.* No Western country came remotely close to the population and resources of the United States. As we know in retrospect, the Americans were able to fight a two-ocean war, in the Atlantic and in the Pacific. No other nation could even remotely approach such a capability.

But the Americans could.

So given US resources, a frontal attack on continental Europe—to hit the Germans in North-West Europe—not only made strategic sense but, for a nation as powerful as the United States, was something well within the bounds of feasibility. To men such as Eisenhower and his boss Marshall, American thinking was both logical and eminently achievable.

Here we should leap ahead just briefly to 1949 and the origins of NATO, of which Eisenhower would be the first Supreme Allied Commander Europe (SACEUR). In agreeing to the formation of the British Army of the Rhine, for the first time in the United Kingdom's history there existed a continent-based, permanent land force. It was, as we shall see, a continuation of the British invading army of 1944–1945, but when Germany gained independence and joined NATO in 1955, it remained there under a new name. And if the Soviet Union had ever invaded Germany, there would have been a British force already in place, ready to stop the attack. In the 2020s there are still British and American NATO forces based in Germany, and in some cases farther forward still, in the now-free nations of Poland and Estonia.

Within seven years (1942–1949), therefore, Eisenhower's approach prevailed—it is indeed the basis of NATO itself—and as president he would hone that way of thinking further, in relation to the Soviet threat that NATO was established to deter.

For us today, looking back eight decades and more, it is hard to envisage how very different things were then, conceptually as well as anything else. In 1942, in name at least, Britannia still ruled the waves. The empire was at the core of British identity, and very much at the heart of how Churchill perceived the world and thus his own role as prime minister, not just of the United Kingdom, but, as he was to put it to Roosevelt, First Minister of the British Empire.

All that was soon to change. India became independent in 1947, for instance, and functionally Canada is part of NATO, along with the United States and United Kingdom, but whose old ties with the Commonwealth—the empire's successor organization—arguably are very much junior to the more important NATO and G7 ties. The white Dominions of Australia and New Zealand are militarily part of regional defense arrangements in the Pacific, with ties to the United States being considerably more important than the old links with Britain. Indeed, the only remnant of a world with which Churchill would be familiar is the ongoing Five Eyes intelligence-sharing arrangement, in which the United States, United Kingdom, Canada, Australia, and New Zealand are still members.

The idea that Britain would wish to concentrate its military strategy in the Mediterranean, for instance, seems incredible now. But it was not just for imperial reasons—as Anglophobic Americans supposed—that Churchill backed such a view, but as we saw, the whole doctrine of indirect strategy/peripheral approach itself, an integral part of British belief held to long before Great Britain acquired an empire in Africa and Asia.

But to return to the main narrative, in 1942 Eisenhower was a little-known US Army planner, and Winston Churchill was the global statesman, whose heroic action in 1940 saved not just Britain but arguably Western democracy itself. The balance of power between the two men in April 1942, compared to what it would be even as early as June 1944 and certainly by January 1953, when Eisenhower became president, was thus utterly and decisively different.

And one other area in which hindsight is dangerous: In 1942 the US Army was no bigger than that of pre-war Belgium. It was a minnow, and at the time the British and Americans met in London, much smaller than the UK army. We now know the astonishing feat that America achieved in 1942 to 1944, a mobilization of forces surely unique in history in its sheer scale. For those of us who recall the United States as *the* great superpower, the concept of the United States as a minor player seems utterly fantastic.

But in actual terms in 1942, and most certainly in the eyes of snobbish British soldiers such as Sir Alan Brooke, Churchill's main military adviser and the Chief of the Imperial General Staff, such an assessment did no more than reflect the actual truth *at that time*.

There is also an irony to all this. Winston Churchill was above all *the* statesman to understand the importance of the United States. It is extraordinary reading the deliberations of British politicians in the 1930s, including Neville Chamberlain opining that you could rely on the Americans for nothing but words. One of the excuses for appeasement is that the British Chiefs of Staff—army, Royal Navy, Royal Air Force—all correctly stated that the United Kingdom could not fight wars simultaneously in the Atlantic, the Mediterranean, and the Pacific. Come 1940 through 1941, with Japan and Italy entering the conflict against Britain and its empire, that is precisely what the British faced.

But by December 1941 Winston Churchill's faith in the United States was totally vindicated. What had seemed a chimera became reality, and from Christmas 1941 onward, Churchill was planning the war with his American allies. *He had been proved right.* It is not surprising that he could sleep well when he heard that the United States was entering the war—even though victory would be a long way in the distance; at least with America as an ally, Britain could not be defeated. Churchill alone of the British political elite actually knew the United States personally, not just because like many aristocrats he had an American mother, but because he had visited the country and come to know it well and directly for himself.

Yet when it came to the major strategic decisions of the war, one could make a case that Churchill underestimated the sheer power the United States could bring to defeat Germany and Japan. Britain could not, as the Chiefs of Staff had realized back in the 1930s, fight a two-ocean conflict. Yet that is precisely what the Americans had now embarked on achieving, victory in both the Atlantic and the Pacific.

Not only that, but when Churchill arrived in Washington, DC, for Christmas 1941, his new American allies surely gave him the greatest possible gift of all—*Germany first.*

When we think of D-Day, *Band of Brothers*, Bastogne, and the heroic British-American-Canadian progress from the Normandy beaches to VE Day, we take for granted that the United States naturally put the conquest of the Third Reich over that of Japan. And that is what people such as Roosevelt, Marshall, Eisenhower, and others all wanted—beating the Germans before Japan.

But *at that time* such a policy, one that was obviously overwhelmingly in Britain's interests, was by no means a done deal. It was, after all, the Japanese who had brought America into the war at Pearl Harbor. And a possible counterfact that very few have explored is what if Hitler had *not* declared war on the United States? What would Roosevelt have decided if that had been the case? The United States would have had to take the initiative in declaring war on the Third Reich. Since the Japan-first lobby was understandably very powerful as the result of Pearl Harbor (objectively speaking, it is hard to blame them), the Americans would potentially have found it difficult to justify war against Hitler at all. It was, therefore, not Pearl Harbor that brought the United States in on Britain's side, but Hitler himself.

Thankfully for Churchill, Hitler's hubris and total lack of geopolitical understanding caused Germany to declare war on the United States. *This* is what changed everything for Churchill, the United Kingdom, and indeed the entire course of the rest of the war.

And this is an important background, for the British never forgot this. The fear that the United States would switch policy and make Japan the priority over Germany always lurked in their minds as an awful fate to be avoided. This should have given the Americans the upper hand, but, to the annoyance of the more Anglophobic among them, this did not turn out to be the case. Until 1943 Churchill prevailed in the policy debates, and his wishes succeeded over those of George C. Marshall, the Chief of Staff of the US Army. Lest we ever forget, Roosevelt was a politician, and ultimately it was politics that determined the outcome, whatever the logic of the military arguments that Eisenhower had drafted for his boss.

In terms of strategy, Marshall had it all worked out. As he told Roosevelt, Britain and Western Europe was "the only place in which a powerful offensive can be prepared and executed by the United Powers [the United Kingdom, United States, and allies] in the near future." This was because in "any other location the building up of the required forces would be much more slowly accomplished due to sea distance."

Furthermore:

> *The United States can concentrate and use larger forces in Western Europe than in any other place, due to sea distances and the existence in England of base facilities. The bulk of combat forces of the United States, the United Kingdom and Russia can be applied simultaneously only against Germany and then only if we attack on time. We cannot concentrate upon Japan.*

So the Germany-first option was not just kindness to Britain but strategically the most viable option as well.

Roosevelt's chief aide Harry Hopkins and General Marshall arrived in Britain on April 8, 1942, with the memorandum essentially drafted by Eisenhower and his team. The message could not have been clearer:

Western Europe is favoured as the theatre in which to stage the first offensive by the United States and Great Britain. By every applicable basis of comparison, it is definitely superior to any other. In point of time required to produce effective results, its selection will save many months. Through France passes our shortest route to the heart of Germany. In no other area can we attain the overwhelming air superiority vital to successful land attack; while here and only here can the bulk of British air and ground forces be employed. In this area the United States can concentrate and maintain a larger force than it can in any other. A British-American attack through Western Europe provides the only feasible method for employing the bulk of the combat power of the United States, the United Kingdom and Russia in a concerted effort against a single enemy.

Come D-Day on June 6, 1944, this is precisely what took place. And it is arguable that but for two strategic blunders by the British commander Field Marshal Montgomery in choosing not to liberate Antwerp before his brave but foolhardy attempt at the Rhine crossings up to Arnhem—the Western Allies could have been on German soil by the end of that year.

And it is precisely the argument of the last paragraph that shows the great dangers of analyzing the events of the Second World War. We have hindsight—they did not. We now have the full perspective—they did not possess that either. What is obvious as to what X, Y, or Z *should* have done is available to us now, decades later, but was unknowable to the people making such decisions *at that time*. Being an armchair general is all too easy. (In the same way, when looking at Churchill and Eisenhower in the 1950s, we know that the Cold War was finite and ended peacefully, but for all they knew in their summit meetings, World War III and mutual nuclear annihilation was all too possible.)

And with exceptions such as Churchill biographer Andrew Roberts, there is also a misunderstanding.

Everyone was legitimately terrified that the Germans could beat the USSR at some stage in 1942. Remember all this was *before* Stalingrad and the revelation that in fact the Wehrmacht was doomed.

The *main* American plan was Bolero/Roundup—sending American forces across the Atlantic, ready with their Western Allies to invade continental Europe on *April 1, 1943.* That was Marshall's plan—and as Hopkins had earlier advised the president, the full-scale invasion should also wait until the Allies had local air superiority.

The Eisenhower/Marshall memorandum recognized that "[f]inally, successful attack through Western Europe will afford the maximum possible support to Russia, whose continued participation in the war is essential to the defeat of Germany."

And since 85 percent of German casualties were on the Eastern Front, this was very much the case—the Soviets *had* to survive in order to beat the Third Reich.

But it was this anxiety that gave the British a hostage to fortune in arguing against the United States, and enabled Churchill to postpone D-Day until 1944. The Americans, through Eisenhower's thoughtful advance planning, thought it wise to include a contingency plan, just in case the Soviets really were on the brink of defeat. This was code-named Sledgehammer and was to take place late in 1942. As Marshall put it, using Eisenhower's draft:

> *Another, and more significant consideration is the unique opportunity to establish an active sector on this front this summer, through steadily increasing air operations and by raids or forays across the coast. This initial phase will be of some help to the Russians and of immediate satisfaction to the public; but what is more important is that it will make experienced veterans of the air and ground units, and it will offset the tendency toward deterioration in morale which threaten the latter due to prolonged inactivity.*

Notice what Marshall is suggesting: "raids or forays along the coast" designed to help prevent possibly imminent Soviet collapse. *At no stage did Marshall suggest a full invasion before April 1943.* Once more, the importance of this cannot be exaggerated. And as Case Blue, the German counteroffensive of 1942, disintegrated in the killing alleys and streets of Stalingrad, such a raid would of course have proved unnecessary. This leaves us therefore with just Bolero/Roundup.

Eisenhower, as demonstrated by his time as Supreme Allied Commander, understood logistics very well indeed. Much detail is given in his plan on how "men, material and shipping" could be made ready for the invasion. And it was logistics that determined the date:

> *Logistical factors fix the earliest possible attack on this scale at about April 1, 1943. Bottlenecks, as to time, will be shipping and landing-craft, which will not be available in sufficient quantities by the time that aircraft, ground equipment and ammunition can be supplied.*

Eisenhower and his staff had all contingencies covered.

And in fact the number of soldiers envisaged for Roundup was bigger than the amount that actually landed in Normandy in 1944. Marshall envisaged at least a million men to invade France—in reality, come Overlord thousands of American forces would be dispersed elsewhere, just as Eisenhower and Marshall had feared.

On April 11, Colonel Albert Wedemeyer, the planner who, after Eisenhower, was responsible for the American plan, met with Oliver Stanley, a British politician now unknown because of his premature death after the war but prominent at the time and a former Secretary of State for War. What is interesting about Wedemeyer is his Anglophobia (evident from his memoir *Wedemeyer Speaks!*). Nonetheless he was keen to fulfill his brief, and in later years he would pour scorn on Britain for rejecting the 1943 option that he, Eisenhower, and now Marshall were advocating to Churchill and the Chiefs of Staff. (He referred to the Allies as the United Nations, a term that would be used increasingly by the United States as the war progressed.) The minutes of the discussion state:

> *Finally he emphasized that the United Nations must adhere to the broad concept of strategy, viz. that Germany is our principal enemy and Central Europe our main theater of operations, while the dissipation*

of our combined resources in other theaters should be discontinued or at least held to the minimum, on consonance with the accepted strategy of concentration of offensive operations in the European theater, with current defensive operations in all others.

In one sense this should have been manna from heaven to the British. As agreed in Washington in December 1941, the United States was keeping to its Germany-first option, despite the fact that the United States was in the war because of the Japanese attack on Pearl Harbor. But as is also crystal clear, the American strategy was a direct assault on the German main enemy in the part of Europe closest to Britain, in North-West Europe, in France. This was quite simply not the British way of war.

This therefore created a dilemma.

4

An Anglo-American Disagreement: Eisenhower's Blackest Day

CHURCHILL'S PERSONAL CHIEF OF STAFF, GENERAL ISMAY, WAS LATER to express his regret to Forrest Pogue, Marshall's official biographer, about how the April Anglo-American talks in London emerged, the conclusions to which were soon to make all the difference on how Eisenhower would command the war.

On the one hand, Germany-first was magnificent good news. On the other hand, if they seriously alienated their new and powerful ally, Churchill and his commanders were fully aware that the United States could switch to a Japan-first option, out of anger over British refusal to go along with the American plan. Since the US Navy was keen to transfer the thrust of the war to the Pacific, Ismay was right to be concerned.

To his regret, the British essentially dissembled, with the Chiefs of Staff writing to Marshall on April 13 that as "regards the long term view we agree entirely that plans should be prepared for major operations on the Continent by British and American forces in 1943 on the lines prepared in your paper." This was of course Roundup, not the invasion of Sicily, which is what actually took place that year.

To be fair to Churchill, he thought that all sorts of things were possible, and all at once. This is plain from a memorandum that he wrote in December 1941 in preparation for his talks in Washington, DC, with Roosevelt and Marshall. It is a wonderful example of magical thinking— Sir Alan Brooke wrote in his diary throughout the war that he spent an inordinate amount of time trying to persuade Churchill out of ludicrous and utterly unrealistic adventures, the wildest of which was Jupiter, a plan to invade Scandinavia via Norway, which Churchill continued to defend even in his wartime accounts (*The Hinge of Fate*).

As Churchill put it:

We have, therefore, to prepare for the liberation of the captive countries of Western and Southern Europe by the landing at suitable points, successively or simultaneously, of British and American armies strong enough to enable the conquered peoples to revolt . . . if adequate and suitably equipped forces were landed in several of the following countries, namely Norway, Denmark, Holland, Belgium, the French Channel coasts and the French Atlantic coasts, as well as Italy and possibly the Balkans.

Churchill was consistent throughout the war—he never lost his allegiance to the great tradition of the *indirect approach*. Not only was the war in Italy very much one of his choosing when it began in 1943, but he would continue to argue for an attack through the Balkans right until 1945. This was a man who stuck resolutely to his beliefs, including, to Brooke's despair, that ten impossible things were possible simultaneously. And this is why the consensus is right: Churchill was in fact *not* dissembling, as he truly thought that everything could be done regardless of what the military truth might be. For a long time he insisted that the Allies could invade northern Africa, take Sicily, and launch the invasion of Italy at the same time while assuring the Americans they could have the landings in Normandy that they wanted.

(Not everyone is as generous to Churchill as your author: The Israeli historian Tuvia Ben-Moshe in his revisionist book *Churchill: Strategy and History* takes a more severe interpretation.)

But the American military had their own strongly held opinions as well. Field Marshal Sir John Dill, the British military representative in Washington, DC, wrote to Churchill that Marshall believed that with Germany so deeply mired on the Eastern Front, "if we do not take advantage of her present preoccupation we shall find ourselves with a Germany so strong in the West that no invasion of the Continent will be possible."

As Marshall himself summed up one of the discussions in April 1942:

Finally he said he was anxious that the dispersion of forces should be reduced to a minimum. To what extent might it be necessary to send more forces to the Middle East and India? [The issue of the safety of India was of major concern to both Churchill and the Chiefs of Staff.] He thought it essential that our main project, i.e. operations on the Continent, should not be reduced to the status of a "residuary legatee" for whom nothing was left.

By this time the Americans were getting desperate!

One of Marshall's team put it bluntly to the British on April 16:

To achieve the defeat of Germany we must get ashore on the Continent and fight them. Planning for this must start now. The forces for this must be sufficient not only to get ashore, but also to exploit the success thus achieved. The United States proposals had shown the forces that they could provide and the total that they considered necessary to achieve this object.

This is exactly what Eisenhower would achieve in June 1944, not as a humble and little-known planner but as the Supreme Allied Commander, and with the small amount of casualties that we saw in Chapter 1. What Eisenhower outlined in 1942, he delivered two years later.

Marshall went back to the United States thinking that he had clinched the deal. He was wrong. Politics, not strategy, determined the next move, and Roosevelt, *on political grounds*, sided instead with Churchill.

Churchill, surveying 1943 seven years later, understood the essential agreement of a politically based decision. If all the troops would take a year or so to come to the United Kingdom, as assumed by Bolero:

But what was going to be done in the interval. The armies could not simply be preparing all the time. Here there was a wide diversity of opinion. . . . It was impossible for the United States & Britain to stand idle all that time without fighting, except in the desert [of North Africa]. The president was determined that the Americans should attempt to fight the Germans on the largest possible scale during 1942. Where then could this be achieved? Where else but in French North Africa, upon which the president had always smiled? Out of many plans the fittest must survive.

This is therefore one of the reasons why the British dissembled. What they really wanted was a plan called Gymnast, which was for American troops to land in Vichy French–occupied northwest Africa and join up with British-led forces pushing westward from Cairo. And this is what actually happened, with the US Army under the command of Eisenhower himself.

But Churchill and his generals found this hard to admit to Hopkins and Marshall that April. As General Ismay recalled to Forrest Pogue:

> *I think that the British were rather in a way not unfair but not straightforward enough. We knew perfectly well there wasn't a hope in hell of Roundup. We would have had to supply nearly all the stuff of Sledgehammer but we didn't say so.*

It was a few months later, very embarrassingly in Washington, DC, that Churchill heard the news of the fall to Rommel's armies of the vital garrison town of Tobruk, Libya. And it was Marshall's magnanimity that led to the British getting the vital supplies—especially tanks—that enabled the British and empire forces under General Sir Bernard Montgomery to win the now legendary Battle of El Alamein in November that year. But in April 1942, the plight of British, Indian, and Australian forces in North Africa was already dire. And as we saw earlier, the horrors of the First World War and the thousands lost in the Somme Offensive in 1916 loomed large, and Ismay reflected to Pogue a way of thinking that has completely dominated the entire historiography of the Second World War, especially one of its best-known historians, Sir Max Hastings. Ismay recalled:

> *We were very, very weak then and the Germans were very strong. . . . Let's face it—we had not got the offensive spirit. We hadn't got a victory to our credit anywhere. Conversely the Germans had had no defeat. They were full of confidence . . . we should [in the discussions with Marshall have] come clean, much cleaner than we did and said, "We are honestly frightened of what we have been through in our lifetime—60,000 in one day—the 1st of July 1916 . . . and we have not got a big population. 60,000 in a day—that was the casualties . . . . We who had survived, had got that in our minds, and "never again" you see.*

The British perception was indeed that the United Kingdom had never won a battle, whereas in fact they had, in 1941. The Western Desert Force, under Sir Richard O'Connor, in Operation Compass, won a large-scale victory over the Italians, pushing back enemy forces by hundreds of miles. However, this is now forgotten, and very unfairly to the victorious British—O'Connor had victories long before Montgomery. But O'Connor also had the bad luck to be captured by the Axis, and although he was freed in time to participate in North-West Europe, his glory days were over.

For important political reasons, many of the victorious British, New Zealand, and Australian forces had to go to try to rescue Greece from German invasion. Militarily this was a complete catastrophe, with the British/Empire forces being routed both on the Greek mainland and then again on Crete. Meanwhile Hitler, realizing the incompetence of his Italian ally, not only invaded the Balkans but also sent the Afrika Korps to North Africa under the command of one of his better generals, Rommel. In no time Rommel had recaptured all the territory lost to Italy in Compass, but was now coming close to possibly defeating the entire UK position in North Africa.

So while it is inaccurate to say that the United Kingdom had never won a battle, it certainly felt like that to the beleaguered British.

Max Hastings has also made clear in his writing that while German troops were far superior to the British throughout the war, that difference also reflects the nature of the two countries—a Nazi dictatorship and a more relaxed parliamentary democracy. And that is surely correct—the United Kingdom is not best described as a martial nation, except perhaps in the quality of the Royal Navy, whose gallant wartime service over centuries Sir Max is right to admire.

Today, however, historians such as James Holland (*Normandy '44*) and especially John Buckley in *Monty's Men*, firmly deny that the consensus is accurate: The British were far more of a match for the Germans than they have been given credit.

If they are right, then Churchill's fear that British forces were simply not up to fighting directly against the Third Reich was mistaken. Tuvia Ben-Moshe, in his revisionist take on Churchill, argues strongly that the prime minister, by 1942, had lost faith in the martial spirit of the United Kingdom's troops. The debacle in Greece and Crete, followed by the losses of Singapore and Tobruk, weighed heavily on him, and, Ben-Moshe argues, therefore his entire perspective on the war.

However, there is a sense in which the disagreement between historians on the fighting prowess of British soldiers is in fact irrelevant.

One of the reasons can be seen in how the war progressed after D-Day. Whereas there were as many British and Canadian forces as American on June 6, very soon afterward troops from the United States predominated and were to do so for the rest of the conflict. These were the forces of Bastogne, of the Battle of the Bulge, which stopped the massive Nazi counteroffensive and within months had conquered the western and southern parts of the Reich. These were *soldiers*. They may have been farm boys or car mechanics in uniform, but if one reads the account of 1944–1945, one can see how they so richly deserved their description as the "Greatest Generation."

Look too away from Europe and at how the US Navy and the Marine Corps fought against an existentially more terrible army, the Japanese, imbued with a fanaticism that even the Germans did not possess. Yet the Americans still won, and with massively fewer casualties than anything suffered in the earlier conflict in Europe by the British in 1914 to 1918. The notion that American forces were inferior to German forces is therefore surely difficult to credit.

Yet this is the presupposition of many who write about the Second World War. One of the most heavily overanalyzed battles of the conflict was the Axis defeat of Allied troops at Kasserine Pass in February 1943. The fact that American troops fared badly is taken to embody all US troops in general, and that a D-Day in 1943 would have resulted in a slaughter on the French beaches. But if one looks at how US troops fought later that year in Sicily, not to mention the heroic war against the Japanese in the Pacific going on simultaneously, this one-off defeat looks more like an exception than a hard-and-fast rule. To make Kasserine Pass an exemplar is to forget Bastogne and to insult the memory of the Greatest Generation.

For the sake of argument, let us suppose that Churchill's opinion of *British* troops is correct. What about those from the United States? As

Tuvia Ben-Moshe is surely correct to point out, the "only basis for his [i.e., Churchill's] corollary assessment of the US Army was the preconceptions common among the British elite, one of which was that the US Army could be better than the British." The Americans proved early on in fighting in the Pacific that they fully and equally matched the Japanese. And even with Kasserine Pass, it took almost no time for the US forces to regain their losses. But as Tuvia Ben-Moshe reminds us, "[T]he roots of the British denigration of the Americans ran too deep."

During these discussions, Eisenhower was only personally involved toward the end, when the decision to back Churchill's wish to concentrate on North Africa had in effect been made already. And a series of events was now to take place that would change his life immeasurably and, as *Band of Brothers* author Stephen Ambrose puts it, put him on the path to the White House.

Marshall had been unhappy about the quality of the American military delegation in the United Kingdom, led by Major General James Chaney. He therefore sent Eisenhower to Britain at the end of May 1942 to investigate the situation.

Eisenhower, too, became unsure of Chaney and recommended to Marshall that Chaney be replaced. He also made various suggestions about possible officers to go instead, and to his enormous surprise Marshall chose him to be the successor. As Eisenhower put it, he was now in charge of the "whole shebang." He was now the commander of the European Theater of Operations.

Eisenhower had been chaffing at the bit for some while as a staff officer, longing to have field command instead. Now he had it. But the path to the White House was entirely unforeseen by this promotion. His biographers agree that, in June 1942, the presumption was that eventual command of US forces in Europe would go to Marshall, with Eisenhower as his likely Chief of Staff. No one could then have imagined what actually happened—the Supreme Allied Command going to Eisenhower, and from that global fame and in 1953 the White House itself.

In July Eisenhower, having done everything possible to argue both for Sledgehammer, Bolero, and Roundup, discovered that the British had given their final rejection of Sledgehammer.

In the end the decision was made by Roosevelt, and for political reasons, not strategic or military. (This again is why *military* choices should always be seen in their *political* contexts, and not just in democracies: We know Hitler dictated strategy, to catastrophic effect, during the war, and that however good Marshal Zhukov was as a battlefield commander, it was always Stalin who made the final choice.)

Roosevelt realized what Marshall and Eisenhower did not. American soldiers not only had to fight against the Germans, but also *be seen by the American public to be fighting the Germans*. And most conveniently for Roosevelt, Churchill's plan, Gymnast, to invade northwest Africa enabled the president to sell immediate action by the United States against Germany to Congress and to the American people. US forces would now be in action at the beginning of 1943 rather than undergoing the slow Bolero buildup with all action postponed by at least a year (April 1942 to April 1943). So for reasons of good electoral politics, the president took Churchill's plan off the shelf and adapted it for American use.

Marshall felt profoundly betrayed by what he believed was sheer British dishonesty. In fact, Churchill continued to believe that both Gymnast and Roundup were possible, and in the same year! Logistically this was an utter nonstarter, as the Americans, such as Marshall and Eisenhower, understood fully. If there was to be an American-led invasion of northern Africa, then realistically that ruled out an invasion of North-West Europe completely.

In July both Marshall and his naval counterpart, Admiral King, went to see President Roosevelt in person. Marshall was angry—and Eisenhower at that time agreed, as evinced by the diary quote with which this chapter began, calling Roosevelt's decision the "blackest day in history" on July 22. So furious indeed was Marshall that he was now even prepared to give up the sacred Germany-first strategy and give in to the demands of the US Navy to grant priority to the Pacific. As Mark Stoler, one of Marshall's biographers and a leading American authority on the Second World War, puts it:

> *Marshall was incensed. Disagreeing vehemently with such reasoning and convinced the British were guilty of manipulation and a breach of*

faith, he pushed for a showdown by suggesting to Admiral King that they threaten a Pacific-first strategy if London vetoed Sledgehammer and insisted on Gymnast.

This placed two senior American officers on the same side, since they now argued (Stoler continues, quoting them):

If the United States were forced to engage "in any other operation than forceful, unswerving full alliance to the full Bolero plans" they advised the president, "we should turn to the Pacific and strike decisively against Japan, in other words assume a defensive attitude against Germany . . . and use all available means in the Pacific."

This was in itself a betrayal of the entire Germany-first strategy in which Eisenhower and others had planned and believed for a long time. It is not surprising that Eisenhower was upset.

Stoler is surely right, therefore, when he recounts:

Roosevelt was appalled. "My first impression," he bluntly informed them, "is that this is exactly what the Germans hoped the United States would do following Pearl Harbor." He rejected their proposal and ordered them to meet with him and prepare to depart for another conference in London, accompanied by Hopkins, during which they would have to agree with Gymnast if the British rejected Sledgehammer. For emphasis he signed their directive "Commander in Chief" instead of "President."

Roosevelt had spoken!

The difference, as an American historian wrote on the seventieth anniversary of D-Day in 2014, was cultural—two countries with very different histories:

And there is still historical jousting over the timing of D-Day: If only the British had agreed to invade earlier, all of Germany might have fallen into Anglo-American hands. If only the Americans had been

better prepared for war, the Iron Curtain might have been rolled east-
ward. If only Franklin Roosevelt and Winston Churchill had thought
more clearly, the bloody campaigns of North Africa (in 1942) and
Sicily and Italy (in 1943) might have been avoided.

A large number of Americans might believe these innumerable what-ifs, but not the British. For behind the controversy of D-Day are some conveniently forgotten truths: In 1941, when the United States entered the war, the British had been fighting the Germans since 1939. The British knew the Germans well, having fought them in France twenty years before—where they'd lost nearly a million men. For the Americans the term "lost" was a kind of conceit, denoting a generation searching for a future, but for the British the term was real. After the war to end all wars, the young men of Britain were not a part of the "lost generation"; they were simply gone. They were gone to graves in France in a war that was the worst the world had ever seen. The British weren't about to let that happen again.

History was, in 1944, to prove the Americans right—just look at any cemetery in an English town or village—and the dead of 1914 to 1918 massively outnumber those who died from 1939 to 1945. But, of course, Eisenhower and Marshall could not prove to Brooke and Churchill something that lay in the future.

Despite the efforts of the keepers of the flame to shut down the debate, there are still brave historians ready to face the wrath of those who do not brook disagreement. The problem, of course, is that in reality it is one counterfactual against another. In reality, D-Day in 1944 worked. So any argument on whether or not it should have been when Marshall and Eisenhower wanted it (April 1943), or when it might just have been possible (August 1943, if Casablanca had gone in favor of the American view not the British), is a counterfactual *either way*. The guardians of the consensus are 100 percent sure that a 1943 D-Day, April or August, would have been a disaster. That is an absolute given. Yet if one is fool-hardy enough to doubt so firmly held an opinion, surely the right thing to say is that the belief in a 1943 massacre on the beaches is as reasonable as the belief of those who say that Marshall and Eisenhower were not idiots and just might have known what they were talking about. And if Churchill and Brooke had prevailed long-term, there might have been no D-Day until well into 1945, quite possibly with Stalin having conquered even more of Europe than his forces were able to do in real life. (This is one of the main points of Tuvia Ben-Moshe's revisionist book, for which he makes an interesting case, even if it does not convince everyone—and on this controversy your author is neutral.)

So we are dealing here with *possibilities* and not certainties, if we diverge from history to speculation. As Professor John Moser wrote in 2020, "Whether a cross-channel invasion could have been successful in 1943, or even 1942, remains one of the great 'what-ifs' of World War II. Fortunately we know that the real D-Day—June 6, 1944—was a complete success."

A fascinating and very detailed article in the 2019 edition of the US Naval Institute magazine *Proceedings* by leading war historian Vincent O'Hara comments:

> *War is a complicated business, and changing one variable will have unknown repercussions. For example, the United States cut landing-vessel production in 1943 to build more escorts, and these helped win the Battle of the Atlantic. However, the major military objections raised at Casablanca to a 1943 cross-Channel operation could have been resolved. Had a decision been made to conduct such an operation in August 1943, enough landing craft and trained men to do the job would have been available, and they would have faced lighter opposition. However, there would have been a cost.*

In the Pacific, the US offensive into the Gilbert Islands might have been delayed. In the Mediterranean, there would have been no invasion of Sicily, and Italy may have remained in the war. The consequences are unknowable, but General Marshall was right in his belief that the best way to defeat Nazi Germany was by striking at its heart by the most direct route as quickly as possible. It took thirty months for the Anglo-American forces in the Mediterranean to drive from Egypt to the base of the Alps, compared to the ten months required to advance from the beaches of Normandy to the heart of Germany. That leaves little reason to think Marshall was wrong.

The real reason D-Day was not in August 1943 was because at Casablanca the British refused to consider such an operation and the Americans did not insist. It came down to two different views of how to defeat Germany. One was brash, perhaps naïve, but based on a history of success and a culture of abundance; the other was cautious, perhaps chauvinistic, and influenced by a generation lost in the type of battle their allies were proposing against the very same foe.

On May 24, 1943, shortly after the British finally agreed to participate in a cross-Channel operation in the spring of 1944, even if Germany had not cracked, Brooke complained in his diary, "It becomes essential for us to bleed ourselves dry on the Continent because Russia is doing the same." Historian Max Hastings has written, "[I]f [Brooke's] willingness to allow the Russians to bleed the German Army was cynical, it was a great service to his own country." The counterpoint to this observation is that ending the war a year earlier, even a month earlier, would have been a great service to humanity.

As we just saw, it is easy to understand why British historians instinctively side with Brooke and Churchill over Marshall and Eisenhower. But why would *American* historians do the same? Indeed, anyone who cares about the fate of Central Europe should realize the cost of delay: over forty years of Soviet tyranny behind what Churchill in 1946 so aptly called the "Iron Curtain." Saving millions of people from foreign tyranny would have been a considerable service to humanity, as would saving the lives of all the Jews that were slaughtered in the Holocaust in 1944 to 1945.

Stephen Ambrose in his multi-volume biography of Eisenhower, in *The Supreme Command*, summarizes it thus (Gymnast was renamed Torch when the American invasion of northern Africa commenced in November 1942):

> *There can be no authoritative answer to the question, did TORCH delay the end of the war? One thing seems clear: the only change of the British and Americans winning the war sooner was to mount the*

cross-Channel attack earlier. The risks would have been greater, but so would the rewards. If successful, ROUNDUP might have led to a link-up of Western troops with the Red Army somewhere near the old Polish-Russian frontier some time in 1944. The implications of a Western liberation of central Europe are enough to justify [the comments made by Eisenhower's key aide Harold] Butcher . . . on July 16 [1942]: "Upon the discussions to take place in the next few days may rest the future history of the world."

Ambrose continued, "The speculation can and will go on forever. For Eisenhower, in the summer of 1942, the point was that everything he had worked on for the preceding six months was in the ashcan."

However, all the what-ifs ignore one other possibility that seems hardly to have been debated anywhere—the option to add a US division to the British Eighth Army in Egypt. As Ambrose puts it:

Still, the proposal to reinforce the Eighth Army in the desert represented a most intriguing alternative to the over-all strategy of World War II. The British quite possibly would have been satisfied with one armored and one infantry division, which would have made ROUNDUP feasible. . . . Opening a new theater in North Africa not only required more shipping, it dictated the strategy of 1943 in a way that reinforcing the Eighth Army would never have done.

Fascinatingly, Ambrose notes, Marshall's official biographer, Forrest Pogue, never even mentioned this possibility. What happened is that Eisenhower, while strongly preferring the Bolero/Roundup option, was quite open to sending American troops to Egypt, and to the latter Roosevelt also was open, as he had listed it among the options available to the United States. But Marshall rejected such a notion, and since no one really (except Churchill) wanted the Jupiter (invasion of Norway) option since it was logistically impossible, that in effect meant that it would be Bolero/Roundup or Torch.

At the Casablanca conference (code-named Symbol) in January 1943, it became evident to the Americans that the chances of a 1943 invasion of North-West Europe was now effectively over. The conference dealt with things outside the main purview of this book. But Roosevelt's announcement of *unconditional surrender* is important to note. It was an American idea with which the British found themselves having to agree, which makes Casablanca not as bleak for the United States as many have made out—unconditional surrender was Roosevelt imposing his views on Churchill (who did, contrary to some, know about the president's intention ahead of the announcement).

Was this a mistake, as some have argued? Did it encourage the Germans to fight to the bitter end? And, come 1944–1945, did it make Eisenhower's task in North-West Europe more difficult?

In effect one can say that it really only applied to Germany—the surrender of Italy in 1943 and Japan in 1945 were not wholly unconditional. It sent a powerful signal to Stalin that his nightmare of a separate peace would not happen, and strategically that was a vital consideration.

But it also worked. There could be no possible "stab-in-the-back" legend in 1945 as there had been in 1918—Germany was utterly destroyed, and everyone in Germany knew it. And as Ian Kershaw shows in his books on the Third Reich, the Germans were determined to fight until the bitterest of endings.

Secondly, could a deal be done with *Hitler*? Or, indeed, could one parlay with his associates such as Himmler, who tried to negotiate via Sweden in 1945? The notion should surely be unthinkable. As for historians who play up the 1944 bomb plot against Hitler, such as Chester Wilmot in his *The Struggle for Europe*, the plotters were hardly paragons of Western democracy. Brave as they were, the kind of Europe they wanted to create would not, in reality, have been acceptable to the Allies—and remember, any deal would have had to be equally agreed upon by the USSR, who had borne the overwhelming brunt of the war in Europe. (Tuvia Ben-Moshe argues strongly that unconditional surrender prolonged the war; he is also a defender of the postponement of D-Day until 1944 and rejects the 1943 hypothesis.)

A coup followed by a conditional surrender would surely have led to a new stab-in-the-back movement in Germany. No, the Third Reich had to be utterly defeated for a new and civilized world order to emerge from its ruins.

Casablanca was also the time when two men, each of whom could never have imagined their political futures, met for the first time. This was the first meeting that Eisenhower had with British politician Harold Macmillan, who was in 1943 beginning his task as Churchill's political ambassador to Allied headquarters in the Middle East, and later in Italy. At that time he was a comparatively junior politician, who had spent his own wilderness years in the 1930s because of his resolute opposition to appeasement in all its forms.

Only fourteen years later, in January 1957, Eisenhower would be beginning his second term as president, and Macmillan his first as prime minister. This was, at Casablanca, therefore, an auspicious meeting.

As Macmillan reflected:

> *I had learned to understand and admire his truly noble character. I formed with him a lasting friendship . . . there can be no doubt about his quality as a leader of men. His services to the Allied cause were immeasurable . . . When big decisions had to be made, Eisenhower never flinched. . . . Eisenhower, at all crises, military or political, showed supreme courage.*

As we shall see, Macmillan was a politician with foresight who understood the modern world. And Eisenhower, appointed in 1942 to command Allied troops in North Africa, was now on a path to victory and fame.

5

The Consequences of 1942:
Triumph and *Tragedy*

IN A CHAPTER THAT INVOLVES SPECULATION, LET US BEGIN WITH ACTUAL facts. D-Day was launched on June 6, 1944, and eleven months later the victorious Allies had defeated the Germans, vanquished the Third Reich, and ended the war in Europe. Not only that, but total British and American casualties in the Second World War—including those lost in the fight against Japan—were in the hundreds of thousands each. The Red Army, by contrast, lost over eleven *million* men, and more than twenty-seven *million* Soviet citizens lost their lives in 1941 to 1945. By VE Day the Red Army occupied nearly all of East Central Europe, including the conquest of Berlin.

It was not always plain sailing! Historians such as Brigadier Richard Holmes, Carlo D'Este, and James Holland have all shown in close and fascinating detail that at some stages the fighting in Normandy came close to matching the levels of casualties that embodied the Flanders conflicts in the First World War. But *overall* the deaths among the Western Allies were vastly lower than on the Eastern Front and in 1914 to 1918.

We take all this for granted because what has just been described was what actually took place. We have lived with the consequences ever since—this world that was created by how the war was won and by whom.

Because 1944 represents reality, it is easy to regard the outcome of the debates we looked at earlier as a *fait accompli*, an inevitability that the way in which the war *was* fought was the only way in which it *could* have been fought. The military historians could therefore equally be right, since the actual war was won with very low casualties for the Western Allies, which from the British and American viewpoint can be deemed to be a good outcome.

However, all this ignores the political *consequences* of the war, especially if you were Czech, or Polish, or from any other country seized in 1944–1945 by the Red Army. For them there was no VE Day in 1945; for millions of people foreign tyranny did not end until late 1989. In the West we forget this, but generations raised under Soviet occupation do not.

It goes without saying that it made all the difference when Eisenhower became president in 1953—the first to be elected with the Cold War already having begun—as it shaped not only his time in office but that of all his successors down to the fall of the Soviet Union in 1991.

And by 1946 Churchill had understood the consequences himself. This, as we shall see, was what his history-changing Iron Curtain speech was all about, the division of historical Europe into two halves, one free and one not. By 1949 his great plea had been heard, with the creation of NATO and the decision of the United States to reject the isolationism of the 1920s and 1930s and instead stay in Europe, with a large army through the North Atlantic Treaty Organization (NATO) under the overall command of no less than Eisenhower, the man whose plans in 1942 Churchill had persuaded Roosevelt to reject. The world after 1945 would be radically different from that after 1918, with profound consequences for Eisenhower as president of the United States from 1953 to 1961.

The arguments either way have been best put forward by Oxford and Stanford historian Timothy Garton Ash, winner of the 2017 Charlemagne Prize, and eyewitness to the rise of Solidarity in Poland in 1990 and the Velvet Revolution in the then-Czechoslovakia in 1989 (and a prize-winning author for his writing on Central Europe). The vital point about his descriptions is that he does not look at issues *only* from a military perspective but recognizes the historical and geopolitical consequences as well, essential factors so often ignored by those only viewing the past by analyzing the battles themselves. Yes, D-Day still matters, and so do the wartime conferences, but the long-term outcome does too, especially the loss of millions of Jews to the Holocaust and the forty-four years of Soviet tyranny in places such as Poland and Czechoslovakia.

In considering the two seminal review articles from which Professor Garton Ash has kindly given permission to quote, remember they were written in 1987, when both the USSR and the Iron Curtain still very much existed. *Now* we know that in fact the Soviet bloc had only two more years to run, but nobody knew that even as late as 1987. Soviet dominion over Central and Eastern Europe was still in place.

Remember also that this book is about how Churchill and Eisenhower ended up creating the modern world. The Cold War was the reality they had to face in many ways from 1945–1946 onward, during their terms in office in the 1950s, and for the rest of their lives. But what Professor Garton Ash argues, surely correctly, is that you cannot look for the origins of the Cold War *after* 1945—whether the Communist seizure of power in Czechoslovakia in 1948, or the Berlin Airlift crisis, or the formation of NATO, or any other of the usual dates for when the Cold War supposedly began. No, contends Garton Ash, you cannot contemplate the Cold War without looking at the Second World War itself, and particularly at what he calls "the Anglo-American strategic conferences of 1941–1943." It is one of these conferences that we have been considering in this book.

One could, as Garton Ash observes, take the Cold War back even as far as 1917 to 1919, and the Western military intervention against the infant Bolshevik regime during that period. Could a different foreign policy in the 1930s have made any difference? Certainly Stalin's exclusion from British decision making did not help relations between the USSR and the West, and, with the end of the idea of "collective security" against Nazi Germany, it is not surprising that Hitler and Stalin agreed to the infamous Molotov-Ribbentrop Pact of August 1939, which allowed Hitler to destroy Poland in conjunction with the Red Army soon after. (Here Cambridge and Princeton professor Jonathan Haslam's 2021 published work, *The Spectre of War*, demonstrates conclusively that terror of Bolshevism, especially in Britain, led Chamberlain and others to their disastrous decision at Munich in 1938 to betray Czechoslovakia, with the consequences of which Churchill was gloriously right but equally ignored.)

As Garton Ash argues, the debate on 1943 is not altogether pure counterfactual history "in the sense that the British and American leaders devoted an immense amount of serious consideration to it at the time." Because we know that Roosevelt was to side with Churchill in the 1942 debates, we should not ignore the fact that another point of view was argued by Marshall, using Eisenhower's work, which was overruled not on military grounds but on political ones. That alternative was very real—while it lasted. Rejection had consequences.

The essential point is what Garton Ash goes on to say in his famous article in the *New York Review of Books* in June 1987:

It is important because the fact that it didn't happen crucially effected the extent, justification, and character of the Soviet liberation/subjugation of Eastern and Central Europe. If Britain and the United States had single-mindedly concentrated every ounce of their resources on preparing for landings in 1943, if no troops or landing craft had been siphoned off to the Mediterranean on the one side and the Pacific on the other, if the landings had been successful and if Western armies had pushed forward as remorselessly to the heart of Europe from the west as the Red Army did from the east, if Soviet and American soldiers had shaken hands not on the Elbe, but on the Oder, the Vistula, or even on the Bug, then the balance of power in Central Europe would have been very different—and another 100 million Europeans might today be free.

The consequences of delay could not be put any better. In 1987, when this seminal article was written, one hundred million Europeans were *still* under the Soviet yoke, including Timothy Garton Ash's friends Lech Walesa in Poland and Vaclav Havel in Czechoslovakia. This is what purely *military* historians ignore—the *political* outcome of strategic decisions. Delaying D-Day handed Central and Eastern Europe to Stalin, and Churchill and Eisenhower had to deal with the consequences when both were in political power in the 1950s.

And to make it clear that historians who know their Central Europe are aware of the *military* aspects of the decisions, Garton Ash goes on to say:

If, if, if. The military case for the feasibility of a cross-Channel invasion in 1943—in numbers of available men, landing craft, etc.—is at least arguable, although no responsible military historian would dispute [British historian Hugh Thomas] lapidary judgment [in Armed Truce*] that "it could easily have failed." But we who muse on the mountains above Marathon—and dream that Prague might still be free—have to recall something else as well.*

The Garton Ash view is realistic, taking into account the Hastings view of the Wehrmacht:

> *Even if a D-Day in 1943 had been realistic, even if Western armies had fought their way to the heart of Europe, it is scarcely imaginable (given the remarkable fighting prowess of the German armies) that this success could have been achieved without British and American casualties two, three, perhaps five or ten times greater than those actually incurred. . . . Britain . . . might have lost not merely an empire, but a whole generation . . . as Churchill feared.*

Indeed, Carlo D'Este conducts a fascinating analysis of something we shall consider later in this book—the debate as to who should seize Berlin in 1945—in which he makes an interesting argument on the reason for Eisenhower's decision to let the Soviets take the city. Omar Bradley was worried that American troops could amass 100,000 casualties in capturing the capital of the Reich. In reality, Soviet casualties were over 361,000, or three times Bradley's estimate. Maybe two to three times is thus correct for a 1943 landing—but as with all counterfactuals one cannot tell—five to ten times would mean deaths and injuries above World War I levels, which does seem implausible.

What are surely indisputable are the consequences of the delay of a year, from April 1943 to June 1944. To quote Timothy Garton Ash again, "The war might have ended sooner. Millions of lives might have been saved. Jewish lives. Polish lives. Russian lives." But as he admits, this could perhaps have been at the cost of more British and American casualties. However, "Who can possibly tell? Central Europe might today be a place where Jewish and Polish, Czech and German history could still be written side by side, peacefully in freedom."

But Churchill's successful delaying tactics in the discussions of 1942 meant that, in reality, with D-Day postponed until 1944 (effectively a date imposed on Churchill by Roosevelt at the Quadrant Conference in Quebec in August 1943 and then by Stalin and Roosevelt together at Tehran at the Eureka Conference there in November-December 1943), Stalin won Central Europe.

This is important, as it demonstrates that it was *not* Yalta in early 1945 that carved up Central Europe—what Garton Ash refers to as the "quasi-biblical myth" of how the war ended. The main point, as historian John Grigg avers, was that to Stalin, possession was nine-tenths of the law. By 1944 his troops were much farther to the west, and by Yalta they had already captured vast swathes of Poland. A Soviet official history quoted by Garton Ash said, "The actual potentialities of Soviet diplomacy as well as the role and place of the USSR in international relations and the resolution of world problems were directly dependent on developments on the Soviet-German front." Remember that statistic: *85 percent of German casualties were on the Eastern Front.* To put it another way, what the Red Army had conquered, Stalin kept.

That is why Timothy Garton Ash is correct when he says, "Arguably, Poland was not lost at Yalta, Moscow and Tehran but at Casablanca, London and Washington"—the April 1942 London meeting of this chapter being among such gatherings. As he shows so compellingly, when it comes to Stalin,

> [w]hat can be historically demonstrated is the way in which his designs for (or "on") Eastern and Central Europe develop and take shape in the year between the D-Day-that-wasn't [1943] and the D-Day-that-was [1944], as it becomes clear that the Red Army, having turned the tide at Stalingrad and Kursk, is now bound to advance beyond the Hitler-Stalin partition line. The opening of the western front in the summer of 1944 then precipitates the developments in Central and Eastern Europe that the opening of a western second front in the summer of 1943 might just conceivably have prevented.

Although Garton Ash does not mention the Warsaw Uprising in August-September 1944 in his article, it is the tragic tale of when the Soviets did nothing while the Germans slaughtered the uprising by the Polish Home Army, and forbade the Western Allies to provide any assistance. In the real world, the Allied forces under Eisenhower were not long off the beaches of Normandy when the uprising occurred, but as Garton Ash says earlier, what if they had reached the Vistula or the Bug?

In the actual world, it was ten months between D-Day and the Elbe, so where might an Allied invasion launched in April 1943 have been in August 1944?

Indeed, as Timothy Garton Ash continues, "Only by doing what Stalin wanted—launching a second front in Western Europe in 1942–1943—could the Western Allies prevent Stalin doing what he wanted in Eastern Europe in 1944–1945."

Here again we come to one of the *leitmotifs* of this book—hindsight. For as Garton Ash reminds us:

> *Churchill and Roosevelt did not know then what we know now. The chances of failure [of a 1943 D-Day] were great. So was the almost certain cost in human life. The interests of Central and Eastern Europeans were never the first interest of the British and Americans. Other priorities prevailed. . . . By leaving the "liberation" of East Central Europe to the Red Army, the West made the partition of Europe a near certainty. Given the nature of the Soviet system under Stalin, and the nature of the war which the Soviet Union had fought, it was always probable that this "liberation" would be nasty, brutish and long.*

The truth, of course, is that Churchill and Roosevelt simply wanted to win the war and beat Germany. Churchill wanted Britain to survive as a major international player—preferably with its empire fully intact—and Roosevelt wanted to set up the United Nations and to beat the Japanese, Soviet goodwill being essential to both those laudatory aims.

Roosevelt died before the consequences of his wartime decisions became apparent: the creation of what soon became known as the Soviet bloc (1945–1989) and the Cold War (say 1948–1991).

Churchill, however, soon realized, when his valiant attempts to get a good deal for Poland got nowhere, that a tragedy had occurred: the *Triumph and Tragedy* of his sixth and final volume. Of course he was right. By the time of his iconic "Iron Curtain Speech"—strictly speaking, titled the "Sinews of Peace"—in Fulton, Missouri, in March 1946, he had perceived all too clearly what had happened: the partition of Europe between a free and democratic west and a Soviet-ruled empire in what became misleadingly called by many "Eastern Europe." (Czechs never forget that Prague is farther to the west than Vienna.)

Indeed one could argue, since that speech was controversial, that Churchill in his genius saw the issue long before others fully grasped not only what had happened, but that the results would be long-lasting, four decades and slightly more of Soviet tyranny behind an Iron Curtain that in much of Europe was not just a metaphor but hundreds of miles of barbed wire and defensive minefields, a very literal curtain dividing the continent in twain.

So we come full circle to Eisenhower's reflection that Britain's rejection of the plan on which he and Marshall had worked so hard for so long was "the blackest day in history." It is, of course, poetic exaggeration. But there is a sense in which it was even truer than he could possibly have known at the time.

Can one apply a version of Chaos Theory to the writing of history? (Summarized one way, this states that if a butterfly flaps its wings in Beijing in March, then the weather in the Atlantic might consequently be different in August. It should be said, however, that as argued in the *Washington Post* in 2020, not all practicing meteorologists would subscribe to the predictive power implied by this concept.) Whether or not Chaos Theory is applicable—your author is no mathematician—it can be argued that the law of unintended consequences strongly applies to decisions made early in the war.

This is what people who look purely at battles, tactics, and strategy so often overlook. In May 1942, Molotov went to see Roosevelt in Washington, DC. Through Harry Hopkins, Molotov gained the impression that the Americans *might* be open to a Second Front in 1942. (All this is very helpfully described in the television series and book by Laurence Rees: *World War II: Behind Closed Doors*.) But at that same time, Roosevelt was beginning to be persuaded by Churchill *not* to have a Second Front in France but instead launch an American invasion of northern Africa, Torch. This was indeed the path that he followed, to the immense sorrow of both Eisenhower and Marshall. Stalin felt betrayed, and it was not until Tehran that he could pin the Allies to the ground with a definitive date for D-Day. All this too, one can argue, helped create the Cold War.

Even granting that the military historians are right to say that Churchill made the correct call in postponing D-Day, we have to look at the long-term consequences. (His official biographer, Sir Martin Gilbert, certainly believed Churchill was correct. And in terms of counterfactuals, he would, it has been suggested, have argued that a *failed* D-Day in 1943 would have been even worse for the Jewish population of Europe because the liberation of the concentration camps might therefore have taken longer.)

Here we can make one last quotation from Timothy Garton Ash's seminal article: "The record of Churchill's relationship with Stalin, the Soviet Union, and East Central Europe from 1943–1946 is ... a chequered one." Of the "if's" looked at earlier, he continues, the "greatest lies in the fundamental Anglo-American strategic decisions of 1941–1943 *which Churchill influenced more than any other person*" [my italics].

> *He pushed those decisions in the direction he did for reasons that had very little to do with any vision of the place of East Central Europe in the world, but a great deal to do with a vision of the place of Britain and the empire in the world. After Kursk, and the absence of a cross-Channel second front until 1944, the Soviet Union was almost certain to dominate large areas of Europe west of the "Molotov-Ribbentrop" [line].*

Eisenhower bore no responsibility during the war for many of Churchill's major decisions. The piece of *realpolitik* of Churchill's notorious "naughty document" or "Percentages Agreement," in which Churchill and Stalin carved up much of Eastern Europe into Soviet and British zones of influence, was a policy at which even Roosevelt was horrified, and with which Eisenhower, by this time busy commanding Allied forces in North-West Europe, had nothing whatsoever to do. Nor was Eisenhower party to the discussions at Yalta on the fate of Poland.

But, as we shall see, it made an enormous difference to his presidency, as by 1953 the Iron Curtain was a done deal.

The point here is that the decisions that led to the Iron Curtain and to the Cold War were made in *1941 to 1943*. By Tehran and most certainly by Yalta everything was a *fait accompli*. Churchill realized his new unimportance by Tehran, and his hopes for Poland in 1945 were effectively ignored altogether, as it was Soviet boots on the ground that now counted.

Therefore, the decision to launch D-Day in 1944 unwittingly created the circumstances that led to an Iron Curtain that divided Europe into ideological halves and which in turn brought about the outbreak of the Cold War.

The use of the word "unwittingly" is important, because in 1942 the British, Americans, and Soviets did not know that in reality the war was already won, with the failure of the Germans to capture Moscow in 1941 and the entry that same month of the United States into the war on the Allied side. And to reiterate: Only with *hindsight* do we know that to be true. All three countries had to make decisions based on how they perceived things *at that time*. In retrospect, we can argue that the position of the armies at the end of the war, and the post-war settlement that resulted, was in effect created by the strategic decisions made by Churchill and Roosevelt to overrule Eisenhower and Marshall.

Sir Martin Gilbert, Carlo D'Este, Sir Max Hastings, and Andrew Roberts, not to mention numerous others, all support Churchill's postponement, in effect arguing that the wait until D-Day in 1944 enabled it to be the success that we now know it to be. In one sense, since that decision created our modern world, with the Iron Curtain and the Cold War, you cannot really disagree with history! A D-Day in 1943 is, in another sense, a red herring; considered properly, we can by definition have no knowledge of how it *might* have turned out precisely because it did not happen.

But we cannot argue with the *results* of what did happen, with D-Day on June 6, 1944: Stalin won East Central Europe and all that flowed from that. That is not conjecture but fact. Of course the defenders of orthodoxy would be entitled, with justification, to assert that it could not have been another way. And one could, along with Bing Crosby, "accentuate the positive." D-Day meant that *Western* Europe was saved for democracy. Stalin was only able to conquer the eastern half of Europe—unlike the Napoleonic wars, in which Russian troops paraded in Paris in 1814. France, Scandinavia, Italy, the Benelux, and western Germany all remained free countries after 1945. (Austria saw Soviet troops depart peacefully in 1955, and Finland, while neutral, kept its independence.) Thanks to Marshall Aid in the parts of Europe liberated by the Allies, the nightmare of France and Italy becoming Communist never occurred. And in 1949 NATO consolidated Western freedom and ensured that American troops would stay in Europe and do so permanently. At the time of writing, they are still there.

All this is true. And maybe the keepers of the flame are right: Realistically speaking, this is all that the Western Allies could have achieved in 1945. Given the sheer size of the Soviet forces in relation to that of the democracies, it indeed could not have been otherwise. It is tragic about Czechoslovakia, but at least in 1945 Montgomery was able to save Denmark by getting to northern Germany well before the Red Army. As the saying goes, be thankful for small mercies. It could have been a whole lot worse, with the subsequent NATO nightmare of Soviet troops charging through the Fulda Gap in Germany a reality in 1945. (And here one can surely argue that Eisenhower's broad front approach proved strategically correct in the end, in that his orders to Montgomery prevented the Red Army getting there, and it was American forces that liberated the Fulda Gap.)

But this book does not stop in 1945—the rest of it will look at how Churchill and Eisenhower lived with the consequences as post-war leaders. Not only that, but *Churchill cared about the consequences* and did so very clearly within the year 1945: *triumph and tragedy*. It mattered to Churchill, and so it should, if one believes in Churchill's genius and foresight, as your author does, matter to us as well.

His 1946 speech proclaiming the reality of the Iron Curtain in Fulton, Missouri, arguably, historians feel, did two things. First, it simply told the truth—Europe was now split in two by the fact of Soviet domination of all countries on the other side of the curtain. And second, it was a plea to the United States to stay in Europe, not to go home as in 1918.

He was out of power in 1946, but Truman and Marshall eventually heard him in the United States, and Attlee and Bevin similarly in the United Kingdom. This was not a repetition of the 1930s for Churchill. This time he would be a prophet with honor and very much not in the wilderness. He was both right and believed, even though that recognition did not come instantly. Events, such as the fall of Czechoslovakia and the Berlin Airlift proved him to be so, and the creation of NATO was the vindication of his prophetic genius.

That is why the end of the war was *tragedy* as well as *triumph*. Half of Europe was liberated from the Nazis, the other half conquered by the Soviets, who used the Red Army's military triumphs over the Germans to justify forty years of tyranny in their part of Europe. In fact, many a Soviet bloc city had in its center a Red Army tank from 1944–1945 to remind the inhabitants that it was the Soviets who liberated them from the Third Reich. (Many of these were mysteriously to vanish to obscure places come 1989.) Half of Europe had indeed been rescued from Nazism, but in effect to substitute one foreign tyranny for another.

And no one saw this more clearly than Winston Churchill. But by 1946 the deed was done.

That is why Timothy Garton Ash is so correct to remind us that it was the Anglo-American military decisions of *1941 to 1943* that created the new order in Europe. The arguments in this chapter, therefore, are not based on counterfactuals or on a 1943 D-Day, since we are looking at the *consequences* of D-Day as it *actually* happened in 1944. And it did not take Churchill very long to realize how much had changed. In other words, even if he were strategically right to postpone D-Day by a year, with disaster thus averted, the *political* results were, to so strong a believer in freedom and liberty as Churchill, entirely tragic. His sixth volume was aptly named.

And as we shall see, by the time that Eisenhower was elected president in 1952, he too would understand how much the world had changed. That is the rest of this book.

6

The Most Debated Decision

THIS BOOK IS NOT A HISTORY OF THE WAR ITSELF. WE CAN THEREFORE go from the key military choices of 1943 all the way to the last months of the war in 1945. This chapter shows how the balance of power between Churchill and Eisenhower had by then completely altered, and how the outcomes were thus very different.

In *Eisenhower: Allied Supreme Commander*, Carlo D'Este correctly describes Eisenhower's decision *not* to aim for Berlin his "most debated decision" of his time as Supreme Allied Commander. Indeed, whole books have been written about the choice he made, and it had consequences that are arguably with us to the present day.

This chapter will not go over much-traveled ground. Suffice it to say that historians are now much more favorable to Eisenhower, and the denigration of Marshall, in the lifetime of both men, no longer represents the majority view.

Rather, we will look at this in relation to the themes of the book: How does what happened reflect the changing nature of the US/UK relationship, and did the decisions made have any lasting impact on the world that 1945 created?

Eisenhower's decision on the broad front, and particularly his decision *not* to go for Berlin, still haunted him when he stood for the presidency—and earlier, for the Republican nomination in 1952. That year a famous book appeared, *The Struggle for Europe*, by an Australian journalist, Chester Wilmot.

Wilmot had been with Montgomery's Twenty-first Army Group as a reporter in 1944–1945, so was a passionate partisan for Montgomery's view that a direct thrust across northern Europe could have won the war for the Allies and enabled the democracies to conquer far more territory, at the expense of the Soviet Union. In other words, the end of the war could have been very different, and the fault lay with Eisenhower as Supreme Allied Commander.

The struggle for Berlin could have been another outcome as well. Writing about the inter-Allied discussions of September 1944, Wilmot writes:

Montgomery had now amply justified that the Ruhr was vulnerable . . . by driving his amour 250 miles in a week, he had shown the capacity for movement and exploitation worthy of Patton himself. He was more than ever convinced that the opportunity was there, if only Eisenhower would take it at once, if only he would abandon his "broad front" and concentrate on a "single thrust" to the Ruhr. . . . With 10,000 [of petrol] he could maintain twenty divisions. With twenty divisions he could take the Ruhr. With the Ruhr road taken the road would be open to Berlin.

The book was profoundly against the American way of war, which we looked at earlier in considering US/UK military traditions. A whole chapter is taken up on the will-o'-the-wisp of an Allied attack through the Ljubljana Gap, in what was then Yugoslavia, on which topic Wilmot held the same view as Churchill that Allied forces could beat the Germans in north Italy, thrust through the Gap, and then on to liberate much of the Balkans and Austria before the Red Army got near.

The Marshall Archives are filled with correspondence between Marshall and Eisenhower on this topic, as are the Hillsdale Churchill Papers in the United States, since the Balkan issue became enmeshed in debate over Anvil/Operation Dragoon, the American decision to land forces in the south of France not long after D-Day. On all these strategic decisions, Marshall and Eisenhower were absolutely at one with Roosevelt, who thought that the entire idea of adventures in the Balkans was a complete waste of Allied material, forces, and time. Carlo D'Este describes the notion as "Churchill's impossible Balkan notion . . . a scheme scarcely more than a Churchillian fantasy." In this he is surely correct, and the plan, to which Wilmot gives such prominence, D'Este rightly dismisses in a single paragraph. But to be fair to Churchill, the editor at Hillsdale makes some important conclusions when he says:

The Americans made the obvious point that between Italy and Germany were the Alps. Yes, there was the Ljubljana gap or pass through the mountains toward Vienna, but the Germans might not find it difficult to obstruct just one pass. Allied offensives in Italy had seldom

found it easy going, least of all when mountains were involved. Oper-
ation Dragoon prospered. Operations in Italy did not meet Churchill's
hopes or predictions, in significant part because they were not sup-
ported as he wished. His predictions of Soviet dominance in Eastern
Europe, which he hoped to mitigate through offensives in Italy and in
the Aegean, proved catastrophically accurate.

Militarily D'Este is thus right. There is no way in which such a chimera could possibly have taken place. And the core of American strategy—direct assault on Germany itself—was the only path to victory.
But one can argue that *politically* Churchill was entirely vindicated in his
prognosis, especially as he was proved right by events. Could it have happened otherwise though? Sadly the answer surely has to be no, and this
was the tragedy that Churchill had been so prophetic to forecast.

Despite the sheer illusion of Balkan adventures, Wilmot's book was
most persuasive to many at the time, and to others since, along with the
myth that the fate of Europe was decided at Yalta with a naïve Roosevelt
handing effortless victories to Stalin, Timothy Garton Ash's demolition
of which we have seen elsewhere.

Casting aside Balkan dreams, it is important to concentrate on what
D'Este rightly calls Eisenhower's "most debated decision." It is extraordinary that Eisenhower, in 1952, still needed to defend his decision *not* to
proceed to Berlin. The political misunderstanding of that choice remained
rampant, especially as by 1952 America was still in the full swing of the
McCarthy witch hunts. Wilmot's argument that the West had effectively
appeased Stalin had, in the book's conclusion, the warning that the West
should not do so again. The exigencies of the Cold War were thus read
backward into the policy of Eisenhower in 1945.

To keep to the proper theme, in this chapter we shall presume that
historians as diverse as Carlo D'Este, Andrew Roberts, and Paul Kennedy
are correct, that no D-Day was possible before June 6, 1944, which is
what happened in the real world—in other words, that the postponement
of D-Day from 1943 to 1944 was entirely the right decision.

Could anything else have happened with a 1944 D-Day? Could the
democracies have arrived in Berlin first instead of the Red Army?

Interestingly, as we shall see, it would not have been a British-led attack by Montgomery, but a last-minute move by the American general William Simpson, who to his own surprise found himself just fifty miles from Berlin in April 1945.

Furthermore, as Carlo D'Este shows in earlier chapters in his biography of Eisenhower, in reality *the decision had been made already*. And it was not by Eisenhower but by Roosevelt, as D'Este demonstrates. The occupation zones could, he reveals, have been different, since the president's original conception of the division of Germany would have placed Berlin in a quite different *American* zone from those that subsequently emerged drawn up by Allied planners, those we have today. Roosevelt's personal choice was for the US Zone to be in the northwest of Germany, and in the rough sketch he made, that extended as far as Berlin.

However, he never followed up effectively on his idea and essentially left it to others. This meant, as Stephen Ambrose demonstrates clearly in his book *Eisenhower and Berlin 1945*, that the occupation zone borders were drawn by lower-ranking civilians who had no direct involvement with the war being fought on the ground in Germany.

The result was that the Allies ended up with the zones as they existed in 1945—confirmed at Yalta—but without any strategic or geopolitical involvement by those in the key decision-making positions, namely Roosevelt and Stalin, and with Churchill now very much a junior partner. (This lesser status was very galling for all the British, not just Churchill but commanders in the field such as Montgomery and Chiefs of Staff at home such as Brooke. But when one thinks that by this time the United States had eleven million soldiers in action globally and the British five million, the point is obvious. In a nice irony it was Patton who accused Eisenhower of being pro-British! It is a tribute to the latter's extraordinary diplomatic skills that the alliance held together at all.)

Therefore, to seize Berlin would mean a change in the objectives of the war, not merely to defeat Nazi Germany but to take action to risk war with the USSR as well. This of course was not why millions of ordinary Allied soldiers were fighting. A general such as Patton might be up for war with the Soviets, but few others held that point of view.

Nor was Eisenhower being a simple soldier ignoring the political considerations behind who got to Berlin first. His biographer Stephen Ambrose makes this plain—the distinction between military and political decisions is a false one.

Eisenhower's decision to defeat Germany as fast as possible, while seemingly a straightforward military decision, was in fact rooted in political considerations: This was what the American and British people wanted. His desire to avoid conflict with the Russians at all costs was an extension of the basic strategy of the entire war.

Roosevelt was also against entanglements with the Soviets, and it must never be forgotten that he was relying heavily on Soviet entry into the war against Japan when Germany surrendered. For all they knew *at that time*, that war still had years to run.

But now the issue became profoundly political. Churchill had, since 1942, often written directly to Eisenhower, even though this was basically a British leader writing to an American soldier—he did not send his missives via the political channel of Roosevelt. So when Eisenhower, anxious to avoid a potential clash with Soviet forces pushing their way westward, wrote directly to Stalin on March 28, 1945, a massive storm was unleashed, with the British, notably Churchill and Brooke, venting their wrath against Eisenhower's plan to coordinate final operations against Germany with the Red Army, which is all that he was trying to do.

The real issue was that Eisenhower now perceived Berlin purely as a trophy target. The Soviets were thirty miles from Berlin—*at that stage* no American or British troops were anywhere as close. This was simple logic.

But Churchill saw things very differently, and in entirely political terms. He now sent his own written missile to Roosevelt, who, unfortunately for everybody, was now terminally ill.

Berlin, to the prime minister, was critical. "I say quite frankly that Berlin remains of high strategic importance. Nothing will exert a psychological effect of despair upon all the German forces of resistance equal to the fall of Berlin."

This mattered to Churchill in terms of post-war prestige as well, and here, experts on the USSR such as Laurence Rees have demonstrated, his argument was in effect the mirror image of Stalin, since the Soviet dictator was also thinking in legacy terms when it came to who captured Berlin.

Reminding Roosevelt that the Red Army had seized much of Central Europe already, Churchill continued:

> *If they also take Berlin, will not their impression that they have been the overwhelming contributor to our common victory be unduly imprinted in their minds, and may this not lead them into a mood which will raise grave and formidable difficulties in the future?*

The farther east the Western Allied forces could go, he argued, would be both militarily and politically for the better.

If one believes that the Cold War—the conflict that was to dominate not just the remaining lifetimes of Eisenhower and Churchill but of everyone until 1989–1991, then Churchill is being prophetic. But if one takes what one might call the Garton Ash thesis, that the Cold War actually originated far earlier, in decisions made well before 1945, then all one can say is that Churchill was now realizing the truth *far too late*.

Not only was the Red Army a mere thirty miles from Berlin, but the Soviets had lost what would soon be a total of *twelve million* soldiers in the fight against Nazi Germany, just under *forty times* more lost than those of the entire US Army in Europe and the Pacific combined. The fact was that in Europe the Soviets had indeed been the *overwhelming contributor to our common victory*, and the Red Army and Stalin knew it. (Remember that statistic again—*85 percent of German deaths were on the Eastern Front.*)

Eisenhower left the political in-fighting to Roosevelt, though in fact, with the president so frail, it was, in practice, Marshall who provided the effective reply, as Churchill now realized.

Roosevelt this time, unlike in 1942, backed his generals. Eisenhower was to stick to the plan. The president added his regret that "at the moment of a great victory we should become involved in such unfortunate reactions."

In writing to Churchill, Eisenhower did admit to feeling "disturbed if not hurt," but he stuck to talking about strategy. But to his staff he said that

"Berlin was a terrain objective empty of meaning . . . to send our armies crashing into its western suburbs could have no tactical significance."

As he put it:

> *Berlin is no longer a particularly important objective. Its usefulness to the German has been largely destroyed and even his government is preparing to move to another area. What is now important is to gather up our forces for a single drive . . . than will the scattering around of our effort.*

This was the Marshall doctrine of 1942—get rid of the main enemy, and it was now the American way of war that prevailed.

And this time Churchill surrendered. On April 5 he told Roosevelt:

> *The changes in the main plan [to conquer Germany] have now turned out to be very much less than we at first proposed. My personal relations with General Eisenhower are of the most friendly character. I regard the matter as closed.*

So the balance of power had clearly shifted—what America wanted, America got. No more could a British prime minister dictate Allied strategy.

Furthermore, military logic was on Eisenhower's side. As he told the Combined Chiefs of Staff, "I regard it as militarily unsound at this stage of the proceedings to make Berlin a major objective, particularly in view of the fact that it is only 35 miles from the Russian lines."

He did, however, recognize an all-important strategic point: The idea that Eisenhower was only interested in strategy and ignored the politics is proved false by what he wrote next:

> *I am the first to admit that a war is waged in pursuit of political aims, and if the Combined Chiefs of Staff should decide that the Allied effort to take Berlin outweighs purely military considerations in this theater, I would cheerfully readjust my plans and my thinking so as to carry out such an operation.*

But he was never required to alter his plans by his superiors, and it was the Soviets who lost thousands of lives over Berlin, not Britain or the United States. Eisenhower knew full well, though, that military decisions had political consequences—and also that it was not up to generals in the field to make such choices.

Omar Bradley's suggestion to Eisenhower, that if the Americans launched an attack on Berlin it would cost at least 100,000 casualties, is one that is often quoted in debates on Eisenhower's decision. Less often mentioned, but very clear from Carlo D'Este's biography, is that so ferocious was the street fighting between the Germans and the Red Army, that between April 16 and May 8, the defenders inflicted no fewer than 361,367 casualties on the invaders. Not only is that figure three times as many as Bradley's estimate, but it exceeds the total number of American deaths in the entire Second World War.

And as Stephen Ambrose reminds us, having lost so gigantic a number of troops, the Soviet Union then had to give half of Berlin over to the British, Americans, and French, for their zones of the city. The Allies therefore gained their occupation zones *for no casualties at all*. No American died for Berlin, but soon, as Giles Milton points out in his book *Checkmate in Berlin*, American troops were stationed in the city, and to stay, a vital garrison for the free world during the Cold War.

Just before the Red Army attack on Berlin, forward units of General Simpson's Ninth Army found themselves only fifty miles from the suburbs. Simpson would have loved American troops to take Berlin, a dream he shared with his fellow commander, Patton. However, there were well over *one million* Red Army forces even closer and with secure lines of supply, which the overextended Ninth Army simply did not possess. And as Eisenhower's biographer Stephen Ambrose argues in *Eisenhower and Berlin*, if Stalin had thought that the Americans would beat the Soviets to Berlin—something logistically well-nigh impossible, according to those advising Eisenhower—he would have sped up the assault to make sure that the Red Army got there first.

Simpson was always disappointed by this decision, but how a significantly smaller American force could have captured Berlin when the Soviets were to lose more men in just the one battle than all American forces during the war is a question that Simpson's proponents (and Patton's) have never answered satisfactorily.

The arguments were similar for Vienna, the four-power occupation of which became famous through Graham Greene's extraordinary film and novel *The Third Man*. In 1955, as we shall see, the Soviets withdrew from Austria altogether, and that country, while having to stay neutral, has been a democracy to this day. The fact that the Soviets got to Vienna first made no difference, and Churchill's fears for that nation were unwarranted.

For Prague, and for the people of Czechoslovakia, it was alas a very different story. Patton could easily have taken Prague if not most of the territory of the German Protectorate of Bohemia and Moravia, and prevented the Red Army from "liberating" the country. Once the Soviets were there, they stayed, crushing the wish of that nation's people to be free when they destroyed the Prague Spring of 1968, and not leaving until 1989, forty-four years after they arrived in 1945.

The Czech underground rose up when they saw how near Patton's forces were to Prague, and they asked for aid. None came, to Patton's profound regret, and it was the Red Army that arrived instead. In February 1948 the Communists in the Czechoslovak government launched a coup, seized control of the country, and maintained absolute power until the Velvet Revolution in 1989.

Today Czechs regret what did *not* happen in 1945, and authoritative historians such as Timothy Garton Ash—an eyewitness to Central Europe in the 1980s—joins them in wishing the West had taken Prague, while making the interesting caveat that in such an instance the Soviets might have made trouble for the Allies in Berlin. It is certainly true that the USSR used the Red Army's success as a justification for four decades of tyranny and foreign oppression, which would not have happened if Patton had arrived there first.

Ultimately it is impossible to know about Czechoslovakia, as that takes us back to the counterfactuals we have abjured in this chapter. Unlike with Berlin there would not have been vast casualties if Patton had taken the city in place of the Red Army, but the USSR would undoubtedly have done all it could to steer Czechoslovakia in a Communist direction regardless. Since that country was a democracy from

1918 to 1939—unlike Poland—it is arguable that the betrayal of Czecho-slovakia should vex us the most, the baleful legacy of Neville Chamberlain, because the country was, in effect, under alien rule for five decades (1939–1989).

But in May 1945 the Soviet Union was still an ally, the country that had suffered the most from Nazi evil: *twenty-seven million deaths*, civilian and military, between the launch of Barbarossa and D-Day. The Western Allies, Eisenhower very much among them, were more than aware of the disproportionate sacrifice the Soviets had made. Later, Eisenhower was to see the USSR in a different light, as did the new president of the United States, Harry Truman. But in looking at how people perceived issues *at that time*, the idea of a clash between the armies of the democracies and that of the Soviet Union remained unthinkable. If Stalin wanted to get to Berlin first, and also Prague, that was his privilege, and America would stick to the agreement made with him.

In *retrospect* the Prague decision led to tragedy—the Communist seizure of power in 1948, followed so soon after that year by the Soviet blockade of Berlin—and were the triggers for what we now call the Cold War. But as we have seen, one can more sensibly argue that the real causes of the Cold War go back even further still, maybe to 1917, but certainly to the 1930s and the *early* phases of the Second World War.

Wilmot's *Struggle for Europe* reflects the anxieties of the late 1940s and the era of the Korean War, with that conflict still in full swing when he wrote his book. Sadly, though, he misses one of the key pointers to when the Cold War *really* started, long before the military decisions by Eisenhower and Marshall that he so decries. He describes a conversation at Yalta:

> *During an after-dinner conversation at Yalta Stalin explained that he would not have entered into a Non-Aggression Pact with Hitler in 1939, had it not been for the Munich agreement of the previous year. This agreement, and Russia's exclusion from the discussions which led to it, were interpreted in the Kremlin as a deliberate attempt to turn Hitler eastward into conflict with the Soviet Union.*

We now know, from the archives to which Wilmot did not live long enough to gain access, that this is entirely mistaken. But a historian such as Jonathan Haslam, who understands Russian and has read both British and Soviet archives, argues that the real problem was in fact virulent anti-Communism, especially in Britain, and in particular in Neville Chamberlain himself.

Haslam's book, *The Spectre of War*, published nearly seventy years after Wilmot's, shows this beyond peradventure. Hitler only had to fight a one-front war in 1939 because of what Chamberlain did in 1938–1939. This is why the war was fought as it was, with the USSR entering the war because of the ideological and delusional belief by Adolf Hitler that he could conquer the Soviet Union within weeks, with the catastrophic results that we all know. The world of 1945 was thus not the fault of Roosevelt or Eisenhower, but the legacy of how Chamberlain's decisions in 1938 caused the circumstances in which war began in 1939 and the appalling hand that he bequeathed to Churchill in 1940.

So in 1944–1945 Eisenhower found himself coping with the results of those earlier decisions, and the need to deal with the issues accordingly. *At that time* he could see no way around the realities of whose armies were where in April-May 1945, and the urgent need to finish the war as soon as possible.

Finally, is it possible to contend that Eisenhower was simply being responsible? While Stalin and his marshals were unconcerned about high death counts in the Red Army, all the Allied commanders wanted to win the war and to do so quickly, not just for the sake of beating Nazi Germany, but to do so in a way that led to as few casualties as possible. Eisenhower was such a man and, for all his many faults, so too was Montgomery, whose memories of the carnage of the First World War remained with him and indeed with all British and American leaders who had been junior officers who survived the trenches. Hitler or Stalin might not care, but civilized Western generals always did. No objective was worth one hundred thousand casualties if there was some other way to achieve the goal.

And connected to that wish to behave responsibly is the specter in the minds of Eisenhower and other commanders: the unfinished war with

Japan. Wilmot mentions the fear of Marshall and the American leadership that the United States could suffer *a million* casualties invading the Japanese home island. This figure is in fact well over three times the amount of casualties suffered by the United States in the whole of the war up to and including 1945. A death toll of that magnitude, while tiny compared to the actual figure of twelve million Soviet casualties, remains horrific. And many a soldier who had survived the war in Europe, lived to see VE Day, could find himself in the Pacific, with the prospect of death far higher against Japan than in the bocage hedgerows of Normandy.

This being the case, can one not say that Eisenhower and Marshall were not also being responsible for the kind of war that they were certain the United States would soon face in East Asia?

Iwo Jima shows the fanaticism with which the Japanese fought. Around seventy thousand American marines fought some eighteen thousand Japanese. The United States lost seven thousand lives with twenty thousand injured. Only slightly more than two hundred Japanese were captured—all the rest died fighting. These figures pale into insignificance when one looks at the death toll to capture Okinawa—agreed-upon statistics for this seem to vary, but thousands of Americans, Japanese, and Okinawans were slaughtered in the process.

To the US leadership, such American death tolls were hideous, as indeed they should be to any country. One of the ironies of the debate on the ethics of the atomic bombs dropped on Hiroshima and Nagasaki is that the civilian death toll in the event of an American invasion of the Japanese main island would have been *massively* higher than those who died in both cities, and the amount of fatalities among Japanese military would have dwarfed such figures still further, let alone the predicted one million American casualties.

At the back of Eisenhower's mind as the war in Europe came to an end, therefore, is what would happen to the brave soldiers he had commanded from D-Day to the surrender of Germany. We cannot exclude this when we look at his strategic decision-making as VE Day grew nearer. It was the responsible way to behave.

Of course, if the decision not to seize Berlin is the most debated of Eisenhower's career, the dropping of two atomic bombs on Japan is likely the most debated of the whole war! Strictly speaking, such a debate is outside the parameters of this book, being outside the Eisenhower-Churchill relationship. But the issue of the atomic bomb itself would be central to their relationship as president and prime minister in the 1950s. As we shall see, it would be Churchill, whose military career began as a cavalry officer charging an enemy with spears, who truly understood the full implications and horrors of what an atomic, and then nuclear, weapon could destroy. The United Kingdom was many miles closer to the USSR than the United States, and the incineration of Britain in a nuclear strike became a dread that to Churchill was very real indeed.

But in May 1945 all that was still in the future. While Churchill was surely right to foresee the danger that the Soviet Union would become—indeed, had already become—in the circumstances of final victory over Nazism, Eisenhower's innate caution was surely the only road open to the Western Allies. In terms of Anglo-American discussions, it would now always be the United States and its views that prevailed.

Therefore, one can say that in a sense both men were right, in their different ways. But quite how they had created the modern world was as yet unclear.

7

The Anvil of Justice

WHILE MOST PEOPLE ARE FAMILIAR WITH CHURCHILL'S IRON CURTAIN speech, not so many are familiar with the address given in London by Eisenhower to the English-Speaking Union on July 3, 1951, with Churchill in the audience, together with the then–prime minister, Clement Attlee, who would hold office for just a few more months, until Churchill won the general election that fall.

The speech is important not just because of the post Eisenhower held at the time, Supreme Allied Commander Europe (SACEUR) in NATO, but for what he would soon become, the Republican candidate for the presidency in 1952 and then president of the United States in 1953. This speech was in a way Eisenhower setting out his foreign policy stall—he was still at this stage unsure about running for the White House—making evident his commitment not merely to the grand alliance of wartime, the Anglo-American "special relationship," but also to Europe and the need for the British to be closely involved in the continued rebuilding of the western European nations.

And here we need to remember that although Churchill had made many a pro-European speech, he had not promised actually to deliver what Americans such as Eisenhower wanted: Britain being a part of what was now emerging, post–Marshall Plan, and would soon become the European Coal and Steel Community (ECSC) and eventually the European Union itself. Furthermore, the ruling Labour Party was set against European integration—Clement Attlee would never become a pro-European, and as the foreign secretary of that time, Herbert Morrison, said of the notion of the ECSC, the Durham Miners would not wear it. It was not just a great Conservative missed chance, but very much a Labour one as well—if, of course, the reader is pro-European, which will by no means always be the case.

The speech was called "The Anvil of Justice" after one of its early statements, in which Eisenhower made evident he knew that what he was saying might prove controversial: "Serious differences in conviction must be beaten out of the anvil of logic and justice."

Knowing that Churchill and Attlee were in the audience, he reminded them, "There are men in this room with us with whom in World War II I had arguments, hotly sustained and of long duration." Had these differences ever reached the British and American press, there would, he averred, have been "public bitterness," which was thankfully avoided by these disagreements not getting out into the open.

Nor, one could add in parenthesis here, would they appear in Churchill's own account of the war, slowly emerging volume by volume. Eisenhower was already SACEUR, and by the time the sixth volume appeared, he would be president of the United States. Since Churchill became prime minister in October 1951, the fact that there might be a possible conflict between his high office and the unvarnished truth of Allied disagreements with people also in powerful positions was one of which Churchill was aware.

This is one of the key themes of the story behind those volumes, *In Command of History*, by Cambridge historian David Reynolds, quoted elsewhere in this book. Churchill not merely had a problem with Eisenhower but with Stalin, too, who was also very much alive when the final book drafts were being composed.

So as he confessed openly to Eisenhower (by then in the White House):

> *I am most anxious that nothing should be published which might seem to others to threaten our current relations in public or impair the sympathy and understanding which exists between our two countries. I have therefore gone over the book [Triumph and Tragedy] again in the last few months, and have taken great pains to ensure that it contains nothing which might imply that there were in those days any controversy or lack of confidence between us.*

Not long after Churchill's death, the British archives for the Second World War were released for historians—and members of the public—to read. It goes without saying that the rather rosy portrayal by Churchill proved, at the very least, to be seriously exaggerated. There had been, as we have seen, monumental differences of opinion between the British and Americans, including between Churchill and Eisenhower, essentially solved by 1943 in America's favor because of their overwhelming superiority in weapons and troops. This was the sad truth that had dawned on a sorrowful Churchill at Tehran toward the end of that year.

In July 1951 Eisenhower was still pulling his punches, confessing to his audience that he had made mistakes as well, while not denying the frequently acrimonious differences between the two allies during the war.

But here in London he was out to win friends. He had read Churchill's great pro-European speeches. And he was not above flattery, knowing who sat near him: "Winston Churchill's plea for a United Europe can yet bear such greatness of fruit that it may well be remembered as the most notable achievement of a career marked by achievement."

As SACEUR Eisenhower had met the key leaders of the major countries on the Continent, all of whom would have dearly loved Churchill, with his unique and heroic stature, to lead such an enterprise. When Eisenhower uttered his words, Britain and Churchill could have had the leadership of the new Europe for the taking.

Eisenhower fully understood the vital issues, one that the statesmen of Europe, now contemplating the possible coal and steel community, also grasped as much as he did. As he reminded his audience, "Europe cannot attain the towering material structure possible to its peoples' skills and spirit so long as it is divided by patchwork territorial fences."

This was the whole basis and rationale of the new project—it was *supranational*. Individual countries could not do it each country on its own—pooling resources that crossed national borders was the only way possible. Eisenhower understood this, so did the statesmen of Europe. The Labour government did not, but would Churchill?

Eisenhower, an American soldier, now spelled out the European vision that was soon to become reality, in the best-known part of his speech:

Once united, the farms and factories of France and Belgium, the foundries of Germany, the rich farmlands of Holland, Denmark [sic, as quoted in the New York Times*], the skilled labor of Italy, will produce miracles for the common good.*

NATO, he reminded his distinguished audience, was but young, and needed all the support that it could get. Britain and the United States were essential to the rebuilding of Europe. And as ever, "Freedom must be daily earned."

Now, unfortunately, interpretation and political sympathies intrude into the historical narrative. In his much-discussed book, *This Blessed Plot: Britain and Europe from Churchill to Blair*, Hugo Young in 1998 told a story of lost opportunities, of the United Kingdom missing the bus, and its failure to join Europe at the outset, molding its future from the inside. For those in Britain who voted Remain in the 2016 referendum, to stay *in* the European Union, this tale, written at a time when Brexit seemed inconceivable, describes a tragedy. As seen elsewhere, Churchill's descendants Sir Nicholas Soames and Hugo Dixon were at the heart of the Remain campaign, with Sir Nicholas even having the indignity of being expelled briefly from the Conservative Party for his pro-European loyalties. But to other enthusiasts for and supporters of Winston Churchill, such as his most influential current biographer, Churchill, by keeping the British *out* of Europe, did his people an inestimable favor.

As of this writing, the debate continues! By pure chance this chapter was composed almost exactly seventy years after Eisenhower's prophetic speech. And with one recent exception, American presidents from Eisenhower to Biden have seen Britain's place *within* the very kind of Europe that "The Anvil of Justice" describes, and which, from 1973 until formal withdrawal in 2020, was indeed the case, with full support from the United States. It was not a case of either Europe or the United States, to those who shared Eisenhower's vision, but *both* Europe *and* the United States.

Eisenhower loved the British as much as ever, but he saw—what 48 percent of Britons voted for in 2016—where that country's future lay. He could see the modern world. The United States epitomized it, and the new European gathering would embody it. He wanted the United Kingdom to be part of it as well. To forward-thinking politicians such as Harold Macmillan, who had worked alongside Eisenhower in North Africa during the war, Churchill's speeches after 1945 *perhaps* indicated that he shared the vision. But when in October 1951 a now aged Churchill returned to office, now as a peacetime prime minister, the hopes placed in him by those who saw a strong and united Europe were to be cruelly dashed.

This became clear to Eisenhower in December 1951, when Churchill, back in power, came to visit him at NATO headquarters in Paris. Eisenhower was still in Paris as military chief of NATO, still fending off attempts of Republicans to recruit him for their candidate as president of the United States for the November 1952 election, conscious as ever that he had a job to do in Europe.

The talk centered around a "European army," then regarded as the favorite way in which to get German troops into the defense of Europe, but in such a way as not to frighten the French, who with invasions of their country in 1870, 1914, and 1940 still had every reason to be highly suspicious of their near neighbor and historical foe. Over the next four years, these talks were to prove both exhausting and ultimately futile, but *at that time* they were seen as the only hope of solving the German/French conundrum. And Britain's continued decision to stay on the sidelines irked everyone—as Eisenhower noted in his diary on December 11, from "every side in Europe, I get complaints reference [*sic*] Britain's attitude" toward any such plan.

Eisenhower noted privately, "[I]t is easy to see that the plans presently under discussion on the Continent do not conform with the ideas Mr Churchill has in mind." Indeed, as Eisenhower was to discover, that was an understatement. "Consequently, he is very lukewarm—it is better to say he is instinctively opposed—toward them." His American host tried to put what we would now call a positive spin on the discussion, reflecting that "while I most certainly did not convince him, I am sure that he realizes he must do something in the way of giving us the kind of support we ask."

In reality, while Churchill was quite happy for Europeans on the Continent to coalesce, he wanted no direct involvement. "In other words," Eisenhower noted, "he wants to go back to exactly the thing we had in World War II and merely multiply the number of participating nations (and most certainly multiplying the difficulties)."

Eisenhower then showed that he understood completely the sadly outdated mindset in which Churchill was still living—and, to be fair to the new prime minister, his country as well, since outgoing Labour government would have seen things no differently. In the confines of his private diary, Eisenhower demonstrated his grasp of the realities of Churchill and his position:

> *Frankly, I believe that subconsciously, my great friend is trying to relive the days of his greatest glory. He has taken upon his own shoulders, as he did in World War II, the dual position of prime minister and defense minister. He is struggling hard to bring about a recognition of specially close ties between America and Europe and is soon to depart for the United States in furtherance of this purpose.*

This was, of course, to see Truman, still president. Eisenhower was still Supreme Allied Commander Europe and not—yet anyway—a politician. But his reflections on how Churchill saw him—as of December 1951—would of course change entirely in 1952, thereby utterly altering the balance of power in the relationship between the two men and their respective countries.

But as of their meeting in Paris, Eisenhower was right to think:

> *I am back in Europe in a status that is not too greatly different, in his mind, from that which I held with respect to him in World War II. To my mind he simply will not think in terms of today but rather only of the war years. . . . My regretful opinion is that the prime minister no longer absorbs new ideas; exhortations and appeals to the emotions and sentiment still have some effect on him—exposition does not.*

Within a month, though, Eisenhower was open to being nominated by the Republican Party, while still aware of how much he had yet to achieve in Europe. But duty called him, and in November 1952 he was elected president, the first Republican to hold that office for over twenty years. When he and Churchill met again, in January 1953, the dynamics between them were very different indeed.

8

January in New York:
Churchill and Eisenhower 1953

AND ONCE AGAIN, WHILE CHURCHILL WAS OLD, FRAIL, HARD OF HEAR-
ing and almost certainly not open to new ideas, it is fair to say that nor
were most of his fellow Britons, still living as if Britain were a Great
Power whose leaders could parlay on terms of equality with those of the
United States.

If Churchill was mentally reliving the glory days of World War II, so
too were most of his countrymen, with realistic forward-looking voices
such as that of Harold Macmillan still very much in the minority. In
Churchill's conversations with Eisenhower, we therefore see but a fore-
taste of a political and culture war within the United Kingdom that has
never gone away. Nothing had changed since Eisenhower's "The Anvil of
Justice" speech or the December NATO visit.

In January 1953 Churchill's main reason to cross the Atlantic was
to make his final visit to President Truman in Washington, DC. But he
also decided to visit his longtime friend and financial adviser, Bernard
Baruch. By happy coincidence Baruch happened to live near Eisenhower's temporary headquarters in New York, so that a dropping-by meeting
would seem convenient. John Foster Dulles, soon to be secretary of state,
was also present for the meetings, but the real dynamics were between
Churchill and Eisenhower, both filled with memories from the Second
World War, but now, as Eisenhower realized, talking to each other with a
profoundly different relationship from wartime.

Churchill came filled with expectations. Thankfully for historians, we
also have the very full and private thoughts of Eisenhower himself, since
we have his long diary entry for January 6, 1953, a gold nugget that is all
too rare, as Eisenhower confided his thoughts in considerable and revealing detail:

> *Mr. Churchill is as charming and interesting as ever, but he is quite
> definitely showing the effects of the passing years. He has fixed in his
> mind a certain international relationship he is trying to establish—
> possibly it would be better to say an atmosphere he is trying to create.*

On Churchill's physical condition, Eisenhower was more accurate than he knew, since Churchill's strokes had been covered up over the years. And the great man's deafness was progressing, something that, like many people of his age, he found hard to admit, so that he eschewed wearing the hearing aids that would have made conversation much easier. Things had clearly not changed much from their talks in Paris at Supreme Headquarters Allied Powers Europe back in December 1951.

And now it was Eisenhower who was the leader of the free world, president of the United States, and Churchill, still capable of bursts of sharp intellect and insight, but like Britain itself, past his prime and global predominance.

We do not have anything as intimate from the Churchill side of the talks as we do with Eisenhower's private thoughts to his diary. The nearest equivalent is the diary of Churchill's principal private secretary, Jock Colville, and they are chillingly condescending. Reflecting on Eisenhower and the new team he was bringing with him a few weeks hence to the White House, Colville noted:

> *For what it is worth my impressions of the leading New Men is that they are well intentioned, earnest, but ill informed (which can be remedied) and not very intelligent—except Dulles—(which cannot). Ike in particular I suspect of being a genial and dynamic mediocrity.*

This was, of course, about the man who as Supreme Allied Commander had led the allies to victory in the West against Hitler! And who had just been the first Supreme Allied Commander of NATO! The idea, later popularized by Harold Macmillan—who knew and understood Eisenhower's considerable talents much better from their wartime experiences—that the British were like the Greeks in the Roman Empire, was a snobbery that was to do the United Kingdom no good. And as more critical historians such as John Charmley have reminded us, in Roman times the Greeks were often simply slaves. It is not a happy parallel.

Politically, Eisenhower was completely correct in what he wrote next:

This [atmosphere] is that Britain and the British Commonwealth are not to be treated just as other nations would be treated by the United States in our complicated foreign problems. On the contrary, he most earnestly hopes and intends that those countries shall enjoy a relationship which he thinks will recognize the special place of partnership they occupied with us during World War II. In certain cases he would like to make this connection a matter of public knowledge—in others he apparently would be satisfied with a clear understanding between us, even if these had to be reached secretly.

None of this seems to have been at all apparent to Churchill in any of the talks that took place over the next few days in New York. This is obvious from the formal missives that Churchill dispatched from New York to Anthony Eden. His description of the talks with Eisenhower and Dulles is entirely factual and lacking in reflection. At dinner on the night before, conversation with Eisenhower had been mainly light-hearted banter with reminiscences of days past. Serious discussion, however, did take place between Jock Colville and Churchill's old friend Bernard Baruch. Baruch told Colville that "European unity, in some striking form, was essential if America was not to tire of her efforts—and only Winston (who, he said, was deaf to his pleas on the subject) could bring it about." This was to be prescient of the talks that followed.

Churchill, therefore, as Eisenhower understood clearly, wanted the wartime "special relationship" to continue as a permanent peacetime fixture. But the president-elect made the truth of the situation abundantly plain to his important and aged guest. In fact, one legitimate interpretation of what Eisenhower wrote next says that the "special relationship" was *already dead in 1953*. Clearly, in matters such as the Korean War, whose resolution was, in January 1953, still in the future, the United States, he reflected, "would be damaging our own interests if we should fail to reach prior understanding with the British." But then came the key thought:

However, even in these cases, we will certainly be far better advised to treat, publicly, every country as a sovereign equal. To do otherwise would arouse resentment and damage the understandings we are trying to promote.

No first place for Britain then, surely? Britain would have a key and indeed close relationship with the United States. But would this be a "special relationship"? Surely the implication is no. Eisenhower was living in the modern world, but sadly Churchill was not. Indeed, none of this was clear to Churchill, who described to Eden that there had been two "talks lasting four hours most friendly and intimate."

And the coziness of the Roosevelt-Churchill wartime private correspondence would also now be something of the past.

I assured him that I am quite ready to communicate with him personally, on our old basis of intimate friendship, where discussion between us would help advance our common interests. But I made it clear to him that when official agreement or understanding must be reached, it must be done through those channels that will establish proper records for the future and that will make certain of the proper domestic collaborations that our form of government requires.

In other words, there would be none of the private diplomacy of World War II, in which Hopkins could be an unofficial emissary of the president and issues could be decided in private between Churchill and Roosevelt. This time everything was to be done by the book, and as we shall soon see, this would be to Britain's considerable advantage, as the very informal Quebec agreement that Roosevelt and Churchill had made over atomic weapons was overturned by the McMahon Act when Truman became president. Because Eisenhower believed in acting through proper channels, he would be able to place the delicate atomic bomb relationship between the two countries on a firmly and properly negotiated official basis, as will become clear. But Churchill still did not see the advantages of Eisenhower's wisdom in doing things by the book, being simply glad, as he telegraphed Eden, that Eisenhower's views on atomic weapons were "favourable" from a British viewpoint.

Much of the analysis of the evolution of the Churchill-Eisenhower relationship during this key period has been written by able British historians whose works show a domestic political agenda. This is in particular true of the distinguished academic John Charmley, whose *Churchill's Grand Alliance* set the proverbial cat among the pigeons when it was published in the 1990s, following up on his two revisionist biographies of Neville Chamberlain and Winston Churchill, at which we looked earlier when discussing Churchill's wartime decisions. Even in his postwar policies, Churchill, the great icon and British hero, possessed, in Charmley's view, feet of clay, a view that was, needless to say, as profoundly controversial as his earlier works had been.

In his *magnum opus*, which carefully consults countless archives and memoirs, Charmley argues that Churchill was in fact putting Britain into a position of political weakness and dependency on the United States, and had in fact been doing so since 1941, when the "grand alliance" between the United States and United Kingdom began after Pearl Harbor and American entry into the war. It is a historical *tour de force*, but of course presumes that in 1941 Britain had an alternative path to victory, and that in the 1950s the continuation of the United Kingdom and its empire as a global power remained a possibility. However, all this reflects an interpretation of history that, come 2016 and the British decision to leave the European Union, had profound political implications.

Here, however, it is possible to react in a more nuanced fashion. In considering 1940–1941, it is hard to agree with a view that would have involved a deal with Hitler. In 1953 Charmley has a point: There was a vast discrepancy of power between the United States and the United Kingdom. This is indisputable! So in arguing that Churchill was pursuing a chimera, *this time around* the revisionists surely have a case. There was no way in which an American president and a British prime minister could negotiate as equals.

But the revisionist view has a snag for many who read it, namely that the real tragedy is that Churchill failed to pursue the alternative position that Britain could hold—closer integration with the nascent European grouping that was being created as he and Eisenhower spoke in New York. And furthermore, it was precisely that kind of closer integration of

Europe and the United Kingdom that Churchill was rejecting and Eisenhower was advocating as the best way for Britain to go.

Paradoxically, the revisionists are actually at one with some of Churchill's most zealous supporters, those for whom the great man could do no wrong.

As we saw when considering Churchill in 1940–1941, his *Finest Hour*, one of his most enthusiastic supporters is the distinguished biographer Andrew Roberts, justly famous for the deep insights in his work *Masters and Commanders* on Churchill, Roosevelt, Brooke, and Marshall during the Second World War, and whose recent one-volume life of *Churchill: Walking with Destiny* is now the favorite book for people seeking to read about Churchill in a single work.

Both these historians, Roberts and Charmley, could be placed on what in Britain is called the *Eurosceptic* wing of British politics, meaning that in aiming to join the European Community from the early 1960s onward and being a member of what became the European Union from 1973 to 2020, the United Kingdom made a mistake. And in 2016 this was to prove the majority point of view in the referendum that year. So while one author is criticizing Churchill and the other lauding him, ideologically, when it comes to Churchill's relationship with the United States in the 1950s, both are coming from the same place, despite their very different conclusions.

One of the problems, therefore, is that history is read backward in the light of subsequent British decisions, such as joining the European Community in 1973, voting to leave the European Union in 2016, and departing formally in 2020. Churchill has been used as a political football by both sides in the internal British debate, with speeches he made in the 1940s examined in detail to provide conclusions often of completely opposite natures. While his descendants Hugo Dixon and Sir Nicholas Soames were very publicly at the forefront of the pro-European argument, others have strongly claimed Churchill for the opposite side.

In the twenty-first century, those using Churchill for Eurosceptic political ends have generally been strong proponents of what is now called the *Anglosphere*. This is the concept of the unity between the English-speaking world: the United Kingdom, the United States, Canada,

Australia, and New Zealand. It is, of course, entirely recognizable in the name of Churchill's last great series, the *History of the English-Speaking Peoples*, as Andrew Roberts has been quite right to point out in his book of the same name, which takes up that history from 1900, the date at which Churchill's great work ends.

Therefore, to Roberts and those of similar political commitment, Churchill as prime minister in 1951 to 1955 was making the right decisions in encouraging Europe but not actually being a formal part of it. Hewing close to the United States is the policy that current supporters of the Anglosphere doctrine believe deeply, and during the 2016 referendum campaign in Britain, the idea of a trade deal with the United States, as a replacement for membership in the European Union, was one of the key arguments made by those supporting the cause of Brexit. It is also the view of Boris Johnson, the prime minister who took Britain out of the EU in 2020, and who—surely without coincidence—has written a biography of his great predecessor: *The Churchill Factor*. And it is important to add that in interpreting Churchill as they do, Roberts and Johnson are historically correct—their views now match those of Churchill back in 1953. Roberts's is the accurate portrayal regardless of whose side one is on *today*.

One of the most controversial parts of the campaign in 2016 was when President Obama, on a visit to Britain to see pro-European Prime Minister David Cameron, made it clear that if the United Kingdom left the European Union, Britain would be at the back of the queue for any trade deal subsequently negotiated with the United States.

In fact Obama was merely echoing a thought that had come to Eisenhower back in 1953. Churchill's insistence on the primacy of the Anglo-American relationship rather than closer integration with Europe irked Eisenhower. As he recalled in his diary:

> [Churchill] is unquestionably influenced by old prejudices or instinctive reaction. I tried to point out to him the great importance to the free world of bringing about a more effective cooperation among Western European nations.

To Eisenhower the alternative was Communist domination or "internal decay." But, lamented the president-elect:

To such a thought he reacts with a rather grudging approval but wants to turn instantly to the prospect of American-British partnership. With respect to the concept of European unity, he will say "I have already approved that." But he does not respond with any enthusiasm to an insistent assertion that the United States cannot see any profit in supporting Western Europe economically and militarily unless that region will, through economic and political cohesion, help develop its own maximum power.

As Churchill and Eisenhower were talking in New York, momentous discussions were already taking place along these lines in Europe itself, with Britain, as ever, observing from the side. One of these plans, that of French statesman Robert Schuman (still at the discussion stage in the previous chapter), was now well advanced: the European Coal and Steel Community. The other discussion was about a potential European Defense Force (or Community, abbreviated as EDC), which was designed to help integrate Germans into the defense of Western Europe but in a way that would assuage natural French fears about a rearmed and renascent Germany so soon after the horrors of the two world wars. This attempt failed, but discussions on it were to occupy Churchill and Eisenhower for the rest of Churchill's time in office.

As Eisenhower lamented, unless the Schuman Plan and the EDF worked, both he and his soon to be secretary of state, John Foster Dulles, were pessimistic about the future. And significantly, Eisenhower noted with prescient regret:

One of the stumbling blocks to such success is Europe's feeling that Britain is not greatly concerned and will not help them politically, economically and otherwise. It is almost frustrating to attempt to make Winston see how important it is to the welfare of all three regions— Europe, Britain and the United States—to exert British leadership in bringing about this development.

In speaking thus—and without realizing it, prophetically—Eisenhower was expressing what many an American president would feel for decades to come, right down to Obama in our own times, Republican and Democrat presidents alike. In the feelings he confided to his diary, Eisenhower was correct, as that day Churchill telegraphed Anthony Eden:

> He [Eisenhower] is strongly in favour of the existing EDC plan and army being carried through, and only in the last resort using NATO as the means of incorporating a German army. I said we had done and would do everything to help EDC, but there must be a German army one way or the other. He agreed. We argued about the quality of an EDC army, in which, as you know I have not much faith.

Then Churchill came to the issue that led to Eisenhower's diary entry, showing how accurate was the president-elect's interpretation of the prime minister's mood:

> He then voiced a view which is prevalent here, namely that the United Kingdom has lost interest in United Europe and though he admitted that we could not be expected to join a continental federation, urged that we should try to lend real encouragement and inspiration to the EDC conception both military and economic.

This paragraph could have been written between a British prime minister and an American president almost any time in the past seventy years! In essence nothing has changed since 1953, as anyone reading a newspaper today or watching developments on the internet can easily attest. Britain's conception of its role and the American view of the role it thinks the United Kingdom *should* have, has now, post-Britain's leaving the European Union, in effect come full circle.

For as Eisenhower reflected with sorrow about Churchill and the many issues that the two men discussed that day: "But so far as I can see, he has developed an almost childlike faith that all of the answers are to be found merely in British-American partnership." Eisenhower's next thought was surely accurate: "Winston is trying to relive the days of World War II."

This was especially true of two of the issues Churchill had come to raise with Eisenhower: the British presence in Egypt (Eisenhower had not known that the United Kingdom had as many as seventy thousand troops still in Egypt, which as Churchill realized was becoming too expensive) and in Iran, where nationalists were stirring up discontent against the British exploitation of their oil fields.

To Churchill collusion between the United Kingdom and United States was obvious.

Eisenhower did not agree. Even Churchill now began to understand, as he told the foreign secretary by telegram that day, in which it is plain that Eisenhower had understood his old friend's perspective with complete accuracy:

> *On Middle East questions and also generally he said that we should work together but there should be "no collusion." Contacts should be maintained underground. I said sometimes Anglo-American joint action carried great advantages, even if publicity was undesirable in some cases. I explained in familiar terms my abhorrence of the idea that Britain and the Commonwealth was just one among foreign nations.*

And Churchill then spoke of his belief in the Anglosphere, in support of which contemporary historians such as Andrew Roberts are so right to place him:

> *The English-speaking world was the hope. We had eighty million whites, which added to their population was the foundation of all effective policy. He [Eisenhower] took it very well. I think what he meant by "no collusion" was "no public collusion." I don't like this line of thought.*

Had he seen Eisenhower's private thoughts or understood the president-elect properly, he would have been even more despondent, for *no collusion* is what Eisenhower truly meant. And in the twenty-first century, the essentially Victorian implications of *eighty million whites* jars considerably on contemporary sensibilities. It was, however, at the heart of the still-imperialist vision that Churchill had of the world. Eisenhower's strong defense to Churchill of "the general principles of racial equality"—itself a significant statement in the light of discussion of Eisenhower's support for racial integration in the United States during his presidency—simply puzzled the aged prime minister, whose support for colonial rule remained as strong as ever.

As I argued earlier, one could make a good case for saying that the heyday of the Roosevelt-Churchill relationship was firmly over by the Tehran Conference of 1943, in which Churchill felt ganged up on by both Roosevelt and Stalin—in any grand alliance that might have existed, the United Kingdom was decidedly now the junior partner, the Big Two and a Half, if you like, rather than Churchill's wish to be part of the Big Three.

Eisenhower's memories of those days were considerably more accurate than Churchill's, and he knew full well that a decade after Tehran the world was a very different place.

> In those days [Churchill] had the enjoyable feeling that he and our president were sitting on some rather Olympian platform with respect to the rest of the world and directing world affairs from that point of vantage. Even if this picture were an accurate one of those days it would have no application to the present. But it was only partially true, even then. . . . In the present international complexities, any hope of establishing such a relationship is completely fatuous.

Eisenhower understood, as Churchill did not, the power of nationalism, and how essential it was that Moscow should not be able to harness the wish of peoples to be free to turn them into Communists, even though to give such nations premature independence could, he feared, lead to anarchy. Again, unlike Churchill, he realized that "[i]n this situation the two strongest Western powers must not appear before the world as a combination of forces to compel adherence to the status quo."

Eisenhower's own presidency would not show adherence to this doctrine, with the infamous overthrow of the Iranian leader Mohammad Mossadegh by the CIA and MI6 in August 1953, an event that has never been forgotten or forgiven by Iranians and that had serious implications for the United States in 1979 to 1980. But the principle that Eisenhower was establishing was an important one, and most certainly not something understood by Churchill, whose views on Third World peoples had been fixed in the days in which he was a young cavalry officer in the British Empire at the end of the nineteenth century.

As Eisenhower realized, there was "great danger" if the "two most powerful free nations" appeared to collude in a "take it or leave it fashion." If they came separately to their conclusions, this would be an advantage.

Times had changed, as Eisenhower instinctively understood, but Churchill did not. Nationalism was now a powerful force, the legitimacy of which Eisenhower fully grasped—even though, of course, there would be countries in the years ahead that would wish he had stuck to his principles! Nevertheless, as the two men sat in New York in January 1953, Eisenhower realized that the world was now different in a way that the much older Churchill, mentally still in the Victorian era, did not:

> *Winston does not by any means propose to resort to power politics and to disregard legitimate aspirations among weaker peoples. But he does take the rather old-fashioned, paternalistic approach that since we, with our experience and power, will be required to support and carry the heavy burdens of decent international plans, as well as to aid infant nations toward self-dependence, other nations should recognize the wisdom of our suggestions and follow them.*

All this, Eisenhower realized, would take time and patience.

And Eisenhower could see too that Churchill was what we could call an old man in a hurry, a fate that Eisenhower was determined to avoid for himself, and a promise that he was to keep after retiring in 1961.

> *Much as I hold Winston in my personal affection and much as I admire him for his past accomplishments and leadership, I wish that he would*

turn over leadership of the British Conservative party to younger men. He could perform a very great function by coming forward with his inspiring voice only when critical circumstances so demanded. I am very much afraid that he will never voluntarily adopt this kind of semi-active role.

Ironically, when the successor and younger man, Anthony Eden, did come to power in 1955, he would involve the United Kingdom in one of its most catastrophic decisions, the Suez crisis of 1956, with Eisenhower firmly against him and his disastrous policies. And on Europe, for those of a more *Europhile* outlook, even worse was Eden's disdain for the emerging European Economic Community, with consequences that those of us with a more pro-European disposition would regard as even more cataclysmic than Suez.

But in January 1953, the president-elect was by no means alone in his views that Churchill had gone on for far too long. His friend and wartime colleague Harold Macmillan was still only Minister of Housing, his future greatness yet unknown, his unexpected premiership four years into the future.

Eisenhower's diaries do not mention the discussion he and Churchill had over atomic weapons and on the prime minister's wish to visit Stalin, to help create a more peaceful global atmosphere.

On atomic weapons Eisenhower was most sympathetic with Churchill, agreeing with him that the McMahon Act, which prohibited the United States from sharing its nuclear secrets with other countries, needed to be changed. This is what Churchill had hoped to hear.

On meeting Stalin the news was not so good. Churchill could go on his own if he wished, but as for Eisenhower, he would be willing to meet the Soviet dictator in a neutral capital such as Stockholm—but not with the British present, as that "would involve asking France and Italy." The president, unlike Churchill, was clearly *not* a man in a hurry.

As Churchill lamented to Eden:

I tell you all this to show you the rough weather that may well lie ahead in dealing with the Republicans who have been twenty years

out of power; and I feel very sure we should not expect early favourable
results. Much patience will be needed.

Indeed, Churchill discovered this the night he dined with Governor Thomas Dewey, the former Republican candidate for the presidency. It seems that angry debate ensued. The prime minister went to bed fuming and, according to Colville, "said some very harsh things about the Republican party in general and Dulles in particular" whose "great slab of a face he disliked and distrusted." This did not augur well for a relationship with the new regime.

9
The English-Speaking Peoples

From Arcadia to Potsdam, Churchill had attended some of the greatest summits in the Second World War, perhaps some of the most important in history itself, as their deliberations had decided the fate of millions. Churchill's dream was to be at another such summit, one that ensured global peace and would make the world that future generations would inherit a safer place in which to live.

Sadly for him, that profound wish was never to be fulfilled. He did have a final summit, but the meeting he had with Eisenhower and leaders from France was to be a sad anti-climax to his long career.

The background for much of 1953 was the armistice negotiations for the Korean War, the ultimately unsuccessful attempts to put together a European Defense Community as a way of getting Germany rearmed, the Soviet attempt to get Western troops out of its German occupation zones via the establishment of a neutral Germany (which also failed), and the issue of British troops in Egypt to guard the Suez Canal. All this occupied a large amount of the correspondence between Churchill and Eisenhower.

But an event at the beginning of March was to overshadow everything, and it is on that event we shall concentrate here. Stalin's death on March 5, 1953, gave Churchill hope that a summit might be possible. At this early stage the Soviet dictator had no one successor, and a more collective leadership now took charge in Moscow; Kruschev's ascent to power came later, and in the spring of 1953 it was his fellow Politburo members Malenkov and Molotov who commanded attention in the West.

Churchill was quick to remind Eisenhower of their discussions in New York two months earlier. Then Eisenhower had given permission for Churchill to go on his own, but not jointly with the United States. Now that Stalin was gone, however, Churchill argued, that could change.

I have the feeling that we might both of us together or separately be called to account if no attempt were to be made to turn over a leaf so that a new page would be started with something more coherent on it than a series of casual and dangerous incidents at the many points of contact between the two divisions of the world. I cannot doubt that you are thinking deeply on this which holds first place in my thoughts.

The answer is that the president *was* thinking on how to take advantage of Stalin's death, but not in quite the same way that was occupying Churchill's waking hours. Eisenhower was biding his time. Earlier in New York he had not ruled out a collective approach. But as he had tried to make clear to Churchill back in January, his feeling again in March was that unilateral approaches were fine so long as Britain and the United States kept in touch with each other.

In his reply to Churchill, he reiterated this point:

Even now I tend to doubt the wisdom of a formal multilateral meeting since this would give our opponent the same kind of opportunity he has had so often to use such a meeting simultaneously to balk every reasonable effort of ourselves and to make the whole occurence [sic] another propaganda mill for the Soviet.

He did give Churchill a small amount of hope though: "It is entirely possible, however, that your government and ourselves should agree upon some general purpose and program under which each would have a specific part to play." This, of course, was suitably vague and brought a summit no closer.

During this period much of their correspondence centered on Egypt and the issue of British troops in that country to guard the Suez Canal. Churchill hoped that he could bring the Americans more fully into the discussions. Once more, he vindicated Eisenhower's private thoughts back in January that he saw everything in terms of the Anglo-American relationship. As he wrote to the president on April 5, now addressing him as "My dear friend," Eisenhower would "know the importance I attach to our informal interchange of thoughts."

Even in a letter mainly on Egyptian policy, Churchill began:

Of course my Number One [thought] is Britain with her eighty million white English-Speaking people working with your hundred-and-forty million. My hope for the future is founded on the increasing unity of the English-Speaking world. If that holds all holds. If that fails no one can be sure of what will happen.

Thinking of a joint approach to the Suez Canal issue and other British interests in the region, he continued—bearing in mind Eisenhower's earlier strictures:

This does not mean that we should try to dominate international discussions or always try to say the same thing. There are some cases however where without offending the circle of nations the fact that Britain and the United States took a joint initiative might by itself settle a dispute peaceably to the general advantage of the free world.

It is significant that the American edition of the Churchill-Eisenhower correspondence has to have a footnote by "eighty million," to explain that this was not the population of the United Kingdom but of Britain and its empire. In writing as he did, Churchill was still mentally in another age. The *white* Dominions—Canada, Australia, and New Zealand—were now fully independent countries with their own foreign policy and their own individual relationships with the United States. And Churchill is taking no account of the large African American community when he refers to the United States. But it reflects strongly the view of the world he possessed even as prime minister in the 1950s.

Although the concept of the *British Commonwealth* was to have resonance in Britain's decision making for a few years yet, the concept of a united white empire with a common approach was already out of date by 1953, especially since the largest and most populous country in the Commonwealth was the non-white nation of India. The very next year, at the Bandung Conference of 1954, both India and Egypt would come together as non-aligned nations—neither capitalist west nor communist east. The empire of Churchill's youth, and even that of recent years, had changed beyond recognition.

While Churchill's worldview was steeped in a bygone era, Eisenhower was living in the reality of the post-war world. Having replied to the prime minister on the Egyptian issue, the president added a plea:

> *There is another subject of vital interest to us both and concerning which I have spoken to you a number of times. It is the need, in Europe, for uniform progress on the Common Defense plan and for greater political and economic unity.*

(The immediate issue was the European Defense Community treaty, which had been ratified in 1952, but which the French Parliament vetoed by a clear majority on August 30, 1954, thus rendering it inoperable. But the original institutions of the future European Union—such as the European Coal and Steel Community, were already functioning, as Eisenhower knew and was trying hard to remind Churchill. Of this we do not see any mention from Churchill's side in his correspondence with the president).

In some desperation, Eisenhower went on to say that, after talking to several West European countries:

> *Almost without exception they have said that a more public endorsement by Great Britain of these projects would be helpful. . . . Permit me to say again that I should very much like you to seize some appropriate opportunity to make a major address on the general subject of greater European and economic unity, stating in your own inimitable and eloquent way the things that you have already announced that Britain is ready to do in support of these purposes. Such might just happen to be the decisive influence.*

But the Churchill of the great speeches of the 1940s was no more. What counted was the relationship with the United States, and all else was subordinate to that.

For American readers, the weight of such a discussion will be sorrow, joy, or indifference, since Churchill's decisions have not directly affected the history of the United States. But for British readers the impact will be monumental, again dependent on what side they took in the referendum of 2016 and in the decades of debate both before then and in the years since.

The issue of Europe has divided the United Kingdom like no other—indeed, by the time that you read this, the kingdom might be united no more, if Scotland, which was majority pro-European, has voted for independence. For pro-Europeans, Churchill's lack of interest in matters across the English Channel is one of the great tragedies of our time. For those who support the Anglosphere, Churchill was right and prescient, and Britain's formal membership of Europe from 1973 to 2020 a tragic diversion from the nation's true path. And it is here that we see the fateful decisions that led to the decades in which the United Kingdom was in one sense neither fully in nor fully out, with an ambivalent relationship to its European nearby neighbors that was never resolved.

Yet as will become increasingly clear, the way in which British leaders saw the "special relationship" with the United States, and how Americans saw it, is not at all the same. It was already plain in January 1953 that Eisenhower, while fond of Churchill personally, saw the relationship as being far from unique, if indeed special at all. If the massive economic and military disparity between the two nations was apparent at Tehran in 1943, when Roosevelt so unkindly taunted Churchill, then by 1953, with the far more benign Eisenhower in power, it was more gigantic still. If there was a relationship, it was clearly one-sided.

Churchill was determined to take full advantage of Stalin's death to achieve the lasting peace for which he now longed. He wrote to Eisenhower on April 5 that it "would be a pity if sudden frost nipped spring in the bud, or if this could be alleged, even if there were no real spring. . . . A new hope has, I feel, been created in the unhappy, bewildered world."

His plea was an urgent one because Eisenhower was also about to make a speech, titled "The Chance for Peace," in Washington, DC, to the Society of Newspaper Editors on April 16. This was, as British historian Kevin Ruane has described it, "one of the most impassioned of his presidency." Eisenhower fully grasped the "perpetual fear and tension" that gripped the world, adding that this "is not a way of life at all. . . . Under the cloud of threatening war, it is humanity hanging from a cross of iron."

In the speech he asked the Soviets to give concrete proof of their change of attitudes—the Korean War still continued and discussions on Soviet withdrawal from Austria had gotten nowhere (on that issue it was not until 1955 that agreement was finally achieved). It was, as Eisenhower wrote to Churchill a few days earlier, important to be open to the possibilities of peace "while at the same time never letting down our guard."

Historians who have examined this speech are surely right to argue that a clear difference between Eisenhower and Churchill had emerged over what to do with any possibility of peace. The president was cautious, the prime minister almost naïvely optimistic, taking the Soviets at their word in a way that the Americans refused to do. And within the British government itself, Eisenhower's wartime friend Harold Macmillan shared the United States' reservations, noting in his diary that the Soviet démarche was a cynical ploy to weaken the West's resolve and slow down NATO rearmament.

Churchill, however, never gave up! In telling Eisenhower how well the speech was received in Britain, he went back to his old theme of a Great Power conference. While conceding that Soviet concessions on Korea were unlikely, he went on to suggest:

> In my opinion the best would be that the three victorious Powers, who separated at Potsdam in 1945, should come together again. . . . I am sure the world will expect something like this to emerge if the Soviets do not turn your proposals down abruptly.

And in similar vein Churchill raised the possibility of his having a personal meeting with the Soviets in Stockholm, something he wrongly understood Eisenhower had given the green light on back in New York in January.

The president however was not to be hurried:

> I feel that we should not rush things too much. . . . Premature action by us . . . might have the effect of giving the Soviets an easy way out of the position in which I think they are now placed. We have so far seen no concrete Soviet actions which would indicate their willingness to

perform in connection with larger issues. . . . The situation has changed considerably since we talked in New York and I believe that we should watch developments for a while longer before determining our further course.

But far from getting the message, Churchill went further and now suggested to Eisenhower that he ought to fly to Moscow and meet Malenkov, the key member of the interim Soviet leadership.

This time the president did not mince his words. On May 5 he wrote to Churchill to say that he and Dulles "have considered it deeply and since you sought my views I must say that we would advise against it." The Soviets were bound to see a trip by Churchill to Moscow as a sign of weakness. As everyone would presume that he had sought American advice before going, such a trip would put Eisenhower in an awkward spot. And with France in grave danger in Indochina the French would, the president thought, insist on a "four-party conference," and the time for that had not come.

Just to make sure Churchill got the message, he added:

Many would expect dramatic and concrete achievement from a personal visit to Moscow by the prime minister of Great Britain. Whatever you say publicly about the purposes of your solitary pilgrimage, I suspect that many in the Far East as well as the West would doubt that you would go all the way to Moscow merely for good will.

It was essential that members of NATO and other free countries should "maintain mutual confidence" and avoid anything that "could be misinterpreted." Eisenhower concluded, "Naturally the final decision is yours, but I feel that the above factors are so important that I should in all candor and friendship lay them before you."

This could not be plainer. But it in no way intimidated Churchill or persuaded him to change his mind. As Eisenhower had long suspected, mentally the prime minister was still living in the days of Second World War diplomacy. Churchill's reply shows this clearly:

According to my experience of these people in the war we should gain more goodwill on the spot by going as guests of the Soviets than we could lose by appearing to court them. This was particularly true when Anthony [Eden] and I spent a fortnight in Moscow in October, 1944. I am not afraid of the "solitary pilgrimage" if I am sure in my heart that it may help forward the cause of peace and even at the worst can only do harm to my reputation.

Churchill still hankered for a Great Power meeting: "It is only by going to Moscow that I can meet them all. . . . Of course I would much rather go with you to any place you might appoint and that is, I believe, the best chance of a good result."

And he realized that his optimism contrasted with the pessimism he saw dominating policy in Washington: "I find it difficult to believe that we shall gain anything by an attitude of pure negation and your message to me certainly does not show much hope."

Eisenhower tried again on May 8 to point out to Churchill the dangers of solo diplomacy, while recognizing Britain's right to act independently. Realizing his earlier missive might have been too strict, he ended in saying, "I hope my comments do not offend—I assure you again I welcome yours."

But it seems that the prime minister had the bit between his teeth and was indeed going to take Britain in an effectively unilateral direction. On May 11 he issued what leading historian Kevin Ruane has described as "a new clarion call for a summit" in a speech to the House of Commons. Significantly, he did not clear his speech either with the Foreign Office in London—which he was caretaking in Eden's absence in the hospital—or directly with the US government (although Cold War specialist Klaus Larres contends that he gave indirect hints).

Churchill began by commiserating with the seriously sick Eden. Then, having dealt with Egypt, Korea, and Vietnam (he was later somewhat critical of the French army in his speech, albeit under the guise of being a candid friend), he came to the major issues of Germany, the European Defense Community, and, above all, the subject of a three-power summit meeting.

We can see his Three Circles policy (Empire/Commonwealth, the United States, Europe) clearly in his speech, although as historians have commented, the United States does not appear. As he put it, in describing two of the circles:

> *Where do we stand? We are not members of the European Defense Community, nor do we intend to be merged in a Federal European system. We feel we can have a special relationship with them both. This can be expressed by prepositions, by the preposition "with" but not "of"—we are with them but not of them. We have our own Commonwealth and Empire.*

This was, of course, diametrically opposed to what Eisenhower wanted for the United Kingdom: British membership in the EDC and integration with the new organizations coming into being such as the European Coal and Steel Community. So we have an irony here—Churchill valued above all the Anglo-American "special relationship" while at the same time rejecting the relationship with the Europeans just over the English Channel that the Americans wished for Britain to enjoy.

Then Churchill came to the crux of his oration.

It was plain that, unlike Eisenhower, he was prepared to give the Soviets the benefit of the doubt in these new post-Stalin circumstances. Having declared British policy as being "to welcome every sign of improvement in our relations with Russia," he went on to state:

> *We have been encouraged by a series of amicable gestures on the part of the new Soviet Government. These have so far taken the form of leaving off doing things which we have not been doing to them. It is, therefore, difficult to find specific cases with which to match their actions. . . . I will now, however, venture to make some general observations which, I hope, will be studied with tolerance and indulgence.*

Once again Churchill was giving a credence to Moscow that Eisenhower and especially the strongly anti-Communist Dulles were not. Churchill actually believed that the internal situation in the USSR was changing. He then resurrected the memory of the 1925 Locarno Treaty, which guaranteed peace between France and Germany, with Britain standing as a guarantor.

He asked in essence for another Big Three summit, of the kind that he had had in the war—one that would be "confined to the smallest number of persons and Powers possible" and conducted with "a measure of informality and a still greater measure of privacy and seclusion." It would in fact be a meeting with no fixed agenda. He continued, "It may well be that no hard-faced agreements would be reached, but there might be a general feeling among those gathered together that they might do something better than tear the human race, including themselves, to bits."

Churchill revealed to the House of Commons the feelings of his heart:

> *I only say this might happen and I do not see why anyone should be frightened at having to try for it. If there is not at the summit of the nations the will to win the greatest prize and the greatest honour ever offered to mankind, doom-laden responsibility will fall upon those who now possess the power to decide. At the worst participants in the meeting would have established more intimate contacts. At the best we might have a generation of peace. . . . For us to become divided among ourselves because of divergences of opinion or local interests, or to slacken our combined efforts would be to end forever such a new hope as may have broken upon mankind and lead instead to their general ruin and enslavement. Unity, vigilance and fidelity are the only foundations upon which hope can live.*

Oratorically this surely matches his great speeches of the Second World War. And who could possibly be against peace? But the kind of foreign policy *idealism* that Churchill now advocated hinged a great deal on his belief of the goodwill from the new Soviet leadership being genuine—and that was a matter of some debate, especially in the more *realist* atmosphere of the new Eisenhower administration, as Churchill would soon discover.

One of his longest-standing Cabinet colleagues, Lord Swinton, acclaimed that Churchill had "given a lead to the whole world," and the US ambassador in London, Winthrop Aldrich, told the administration back in the United States that it could well have been "Churchill's greatest performance" since 1945.

This was, as Aldrich noted, a move to a foreign policy independent of that of the United States. The response in Washington was not a happy one—Churchill had called for a summit while ignoring Eisenhower's strong caveats. And there was not unanimity in London either. Perspicacious as ever, Harold Macmillan, who knew Eisenhower well, noted fearfully in his diary that Churchill's desire for a "big game" would cause a "serious rift" both with the Cabinet and with the Americans. The fact that the sick and ailing Anthony Eden worried that the prime minister would engage in "appeasement of the Russian bear in my absence" indeed showed that concern was not limited to Washington.

In his speech Churchill referred to the German chancellor as the greatest German statesman since Bismarck—no doubt meant as a compliment but odd in many ways as arguably Bismarck, with his policy of blood and iron, was the person who set Germany on its path toward aggression and all that followed in the twentieth century. Be that as it may, the Germans had reason to be nervous, since it is possible to interpret Churchill as putting peace with the USSR ahead of the ability of western Germany to stay firmly within the democratic bloc of nations now emerging through NATO and the ECSC.

This is what Klaus Larre argues in *Churchill's Cold War*. He concedes the idea that the main thrust of Churchill's parliamentary plea was for a Three Power summit. But he goes on to contend:

The significance of the speech consisted of two elements: the emphasis on the link between German reunification and European security and . . . the fact that the Soviet Union had justified security interests which ought to be respected.

And this is where Churchill's reference to Locarno comes in, as the United Kingdom would be the guarantor of any agreement now made.

Today we now know, to use the famous phrase of distinguished American historian John Lewis Gaddis, that Germany was not reunited until 1990, following the fall of the Berlin Wall in 1989, and with the strong encouragement of the United States against the powerful doubts of Mrs. Thatcher in Britain and President Mitterrand of France. And Communism had to collapse in Central Europe for this to happen—the abolition of the Iron Curtain.

None of this was clear to people *at that time*, back in 1953. The West Germans, like Konrad Adenauer, understandably wanted the three Western-occupied zones of the country to stay close to and part of the West, and within two years that is exactly what happened, when the West German state became recognized by its occupiers as the fully independent German Federal Republic, the originally temporary creation of 1949 thereby becoming permanent. When in 1990 the German Democratic Republic—the former Soviet zone—expired, it was swallowed whole, becoming part not just of the Federal Republic but also of NATO and the European Community at the same time, symbolizing the victory of the West in the Cold War.

In 1953 this was a long way into an unforeseeable future. Was Churchill sacrificing the free part of Germany to get peace with Moscow, as some feared? Was it, as the wise Harold Macmillan reflected, in danger of being a "super Munich"? That was certainly the concern of many in the United States, including in Congress. As Kevin Ruane points out, "[T]he Eisenhower administration, though publically neutral, privately deplored the way that the prime minister had unilaterally raised public expectations of peace while ignoring the president's April pre-conditions."

The sick and ailing Eden certainly saw its dangers. In November 1954, after the collapse of the EDC project in August 1954 when the French Parliament defeated it, he confided retrospectively to his diary about the May 11 speech:

> *It must be long in history since any one speech did so much damage to its own side. In Italy, as de Gasperi openly stated to Winston . . . it lost de Gasperi the election. . . . In Germany, Adenauer was exasperated.*

Worst of all it probably cost us the EDC in France. At any rate, the whole summer was lost in wrangling.

Eden, in May 1953, was sick and out of the picture. In 1955 Germany successfully joined NATO, with the former occupation forces from the United States, United Kingdom, and France now staying in the country as fellow NATO allies. In the end the failure of the EDC did not matter. But in 1953 the German question was all-important, and with rival solutions, as Churchill's speech made clear. For the United States the EDC was the solution, whereas for the prime minister, as Kevin Ruane reminds us, he "cared nothing."

10

Churchill's Last Summit

WHILE CHURCHILL DREAMED OF A CONFERENCE HARKING BACK TO wartime days of glory, Eisenhower's main preoccupation was of course the negotiations that led to a cease-fire in the Korean War. (The armistice was signed on July 27, 1953, but as we know the war has theoretically never ended.)

So when Eisenhower's response came a few days later in relation to Churchill's summit desires, it was a mixed message for the prime minister's hopes. The French—with their serious concerns in Vietnam and with their own zone of occupation in Germany—were worried about an Anglo-Saxon stitch-up in relation to policy toward the USSR. As we saw from Eisenhower's diary entry earlier in January, this was something to which the president was sensitive. US-France relations were as vital as those between the United Kingdom and the Americans.

So Eisenhower agreed with Churchill that the two of them should meet—but only if the French came as well, making it a tripartite gathering to discuss world affairs, rather than a cozy bipartite summit. (He had wanted the talks to take place in Maine, but Churchill preferred Bermuda, and Eisenhower was happy to give way.) Not only that, but Eisenhower wrote to him on May 21 that he had informed the French and was now telling Churchill "that this proposed meeting is not in any way to be tied to Four Power talks with the Soviet Union or to be considered as preliminary thereto."

Furthermore, the official statement Eisenhower had in mind to describe the Bermuda talks was distinctly bland:

> *A primary purpose will be to further develop common viewpoints with these friends on the many problems that must be solved co-operatively so that the cause of world peace may be advanced.*

This would therefore *emphatically not* be the world-changing meeting of Churchill's hopes. But as a palliative Eisenhower suggested that wives could come as well, and in writing back to the prime minister he was as emollient as possible. Lady Churchill was delighted and so was

Churchill, as he planned to bring his paint-box with him. But the prime minister's hopes that the delegations would all stay in the Mid-Ocean Golf Club were dashed when Eisenhower pointed out that such a venue might appear frivolous.

He did, however, score one success: On June 21 he was able to ring-fence the issue of atomic weapons as a private US/UK conversation only. And he would now bring with him his atomic guru, Lord Cherwell, who had been working the past two years to set up a proper atomic energy industry in Britain, for civilian use for power as well as for weapons. On this issue the "bloody frogs" would have to be outside the door.

One of the most popular aphorisms in British political life is attributed to Harold Macmillan. He was once asked, according to legend, what was most likely to blow a government off course. His apparent reply—now disputed—was "events, dear boy, events." Even if he never actually said those words, the truth behind them is what has made them memorable—the sudden unexpected event that throws all planning off course. Sometimes they are earth-shattering episodes—the assassination of Kennedy in 1963, the fall of the Berlin Wall in 1989, and the attack on the World Trade Center on 9/11 in 2001.

But even less apocalyptic events can have consequences. On June 23, 1953, Churchill was hosting a dinner in 10 Downing Street for the Italian prime minister, Alcide De Gasperi. He started to feel unwell and realized that he should retire for the evening. By the following morning it was most apparent that he had suffered a major stroke. Gallantly trying to continue, he chaired a Cabinet meeting, but it was now plain that he had to have treatment and recuperate at Chartwell—should he recover at all, as he was now nearing seventy-nine years old.

In normal circumstances Eden's longed-for takeover of power would now have happened. But because his operation earlier that year had gone seriously wrong, he too was seriously unwell himself, and in no position to take over as prime minister. Various contingencies were discussed, but what actually took place was a massive cover-up—the Press Barons were told to keep everything quiet in a manner that would seem utterly extraordinary today—and a small political cabal, including Churchill's son-in-law Christopher Soames, effectively ran the country until (or if) the great man was able to return to work. For Eden, who had been longing for years to finally inherit Churchill's mantle, the timing could not have been more devastating, but such was the cruel hand events had dealt him.

This meant, naturally, that Bermuda was postponed, and given the ups and downs of politics in the Fourth Republic in France, by the time that the conference finally got under way in December, there was a new government in power. It also meant that Churchill was able to argue that he should stay in power even longer still, since his dream of a summit had not yet taken place. Once again Eden's inheritance had been delayed, something which Eisenhower, who remembered Eden from wartime, regretted.

On November 3, 1953, Churchill moved the Address in the House of Commons—a speech in which he laid out government policy for the months ahead. (By extraordinary coincidence, this part of the chapter is being written on November 3, 2020, sixty-seven years to the day after he spoke.) The early part of his speech was entirely on domestic politics, such as appointing a retired general to be chairman of British Railways. But toward the end he came to foreign affairs. Compared to when he had taken office in late 1951, the state of the world was "less formidable but more baffling." Fighting in Korea was over, and significantly to Churchill the "United States [has] become again a heavily armed nation."

Above all, Stalin's death opened up significant possibilities. Was there, he asked, now a "new look"? It was hard to know exactly what was going on within the USSR, but he was hopeful.

Explaining his thinking further to the House of Commons, he suggested a view that ties in with what might be described as a *realist* philosophy of how states act—not ideologically but based on their perception of their national strategic needs. As he put it:

> *The only really sure guide to the actions of mighty nations and powerful Governments is a correct estimate of what are and what they consider to be in their own interests. Applying that test, I feel a sense of reassurance. Studying our own strength and that of Europe under the massive American shield, I do not find it unreasonable or dangerous to conclude that internal prosperity rather than external conquest is*

not only the deep desire of the Russian peoples, but also the long-term interest of their rulers.

This was nineteenth-century Great Power politics writ large for the 1950s. And the fact that to him it was *Russia*, not the more correct Soviet Union, is significant—he was thinking about the balance of power between the Russian and British Empires in the Hindu Kush of his youth rather than that of a strongly ideologically Communist state of the kind that he had described so accurately in his Fulton speech only a few years earlier. This was not the speech of a Cold War ideologue, and decidedly different from the worldview of a John Foster Dulles.

Because of his optimism, he therefore wished now to have direct talks with the new Russian rulers. He realized he might be too hopeful—a conference could go wrong, "ending in a still worse deadlock than exists at present."

Realizing perhaps his own great age, he noted, "Time will undoubtedly be needed—more time than some of us here are likely to see." He was in touch with Eisenhower, but—referring again to his own illness—his summit with the president at Bermuda had been postponed.

Overshadowing everything was his knowledge of the "novel apparition" that "overshadowed" everything, the "rapid and ceaseless developments of atomic warfare and the hydrogen bomb." And no one was more aware than Churchill that these were "weapons of destruction such as have never fallen before into the hands of human beings."

Churchill was of course scientifically and militarily absolutely correct: His decades of interest in science had not let him down. He knew that these weapons were intrinsically of an altogether different level of magnitude to any weapon of any war in human history. This was not a new battlefield toy, and in this crucial understanding he was to find that he was altogether different from the Americans.

This was why the United Kingdom also needed a weapon of its own, something explained in much fuller detail in the books of Kevin Ruane and Graham Farmelo, the first a professional historian and the second a scientist as well as writer. For while it was easy to refer, as Churchill had done, to the "American shield," that came at a cost: obedience to whatever the United States wished to do. Within a month, Churchill and Eden would find out from the Americans exactly what that entailed.

Then, in an oft-quoted passage, Churchill invented what in later decades became known as *mutually assured destruction: MAD*.

Ironically, this was to be the best argument *in favor* of both sides in the Cold War possessing nuclear weapons, in a way that Churchill could not have realized back in 1953. This was the argument used by Sir Harry Hinsley, during World War II, one of the key code breakers at Bletchley Park and in later life one of Britain's most eminent practitioners of the discipline of international relations. In essence, if each side knows it can be annihilated by the other in a nuclear exchange, and if both sides are what the specialists call "rational actors," then neither side will want to launch a nuclear strike because the retaliation will inevitably involve the destruction of *both* sides. You cannot win a nuclear war: The other side will die *but so will you*.

This is the essence of what political scientists and military practitioners call *deterrence*, or, more sinisterly perhaps, the *balance of destruction*. If each side knows that war will lead to *mutual destruction*, then they are deterred from using their own nuclear weapons in a first strike against their enemy. They are, in that sense, deterred from initiating war. And writing in the early twenty-first century, we *now* know that the theory worked—the apocalyptic World War III so many feared, and with excellent cause, *never happened*. Books were written in the 1960s and 1970s—and films such as *Dr. Strangelove* or *On the Beach*—that either predicted the horrors of a post–nuclear war or the warnings of complacency if the West were insufficiently armed against the ever-present Soviet menace—the notorious "missile gap" of the 1960 US presidential election.

The gulf between British and American thinking can be seen clearly in the long diary entry Eisenhower made on December 6, 1953. (This is not in the published diaries, perhaps because it was not declassified in 1981? Here we are using the transcript used by Kevin Ruane in *Churchill and the Bomb*, from the original manuscript in Abilene, Texas.) He was now preparing to draft his "Atoms for Peace" speech before the United Nations General Assembly in New York, and he was willing to give the British an advance preview of what he was intending to say. But in light of what he had just told them about atomic weapons being on the table should things get out of control, it was abundantly clear, certainly to Eden and perhaps just possibly to Churchill, that what Eisenhower was going to say at the United Nations, and what the British "knew from yesterday's private talks with the Americans" (to quote Colville), were two distinct policies. And Eisenhower was well aware of how he differed from Churchill and Eden, as his private reflections show.

"The British thinking" he began, "apparently both government and personal thinking—still looks upon the use of the atom bomb as the initiation of a completely new era in war." Here he had interpreted both Eden and Churchill correctly. He went on to reflect:

> *This feeling unquestionably arises out of the fact that up until this time the British have had no atom bombs and because of their experience in World War II, they see themselves as the initial and possibly principal, target of a Soviet bomb offensive. They apparently cling to the hope (to us fatuous) that if we avoid the first use of the atom bomb in any war, that the Soviets might likewise abstain. Our thinking, on the other hand, has come a long ways past this kind of conjecture and hope.*

This was indeed very different from the British position. As the president wrote, "Specifically we have come to the conclusion that the atom bomb has to be treated just as another weapon in the arsenal." This was the crux of the divergent British and American ways of thinking. He continued:

> *More important than this, we are certain in our own minds that the Soviets will do whatever they calculate their own best interests dictate. If they refrain from using the atom bomb, it will be for one reason only—because they believe that their position would be relatively worse in atom warfare than if this type of warfare were not employed.*

Getting down to the personal level of his talks with the British, Eisenhower recalled:

This is one point in which there seems to be no divergence whatsoever between Eden and Sir Winston. I told them that quite naturally in the event of war, we would always hold up enough to establish the fact before the world that the other was clearly the aggressor, but I also gave my conviction that anyone who held up too long in the use of his assets in atomic weapons might find himself subjected to such wide-spread and devastating attack that retaliation would be next to impossible.

This is why the same day Jock Colville was able to recall in his own diary that "everybody was in rather a state" that morning, both about the wish of the United States to be able to use atomic weapons if need be in Korea, but also over the perennial American wish for Britain to be involved in the EDC.

And Colville made an interesting observation, describing the scene in which Eden and Churchill went to see the president to express their grave reservations. The body language was now significant:

Eisenhower was in his sitting room, cross-legged in an armchair, going through his speech. He was friendly, but I noticed that he never smiled: a change from the Ike of war days or even, indeed of last January.

Confirming Eisenhower's diary recollections, Colville witnessed the president give his own clear opinions to his British friends:

The first was that whereas Winston looked on the atomic weapon as something entirely new and terrible, he [Eisenhower] looked upon it as just the latest improvement in military weapons. He implied that there was in fact no distinction between "conventional weapons" and atomic weapons: all weapons in due course become conventional weapons. This of course represents a fundamental difference of opinion between public opinion in the United States and in England.

Eden certainly realized the magnitude of the difference—Colville noted him as saying that if the United Kingdom agreed with the United

States, knowing that America would indeed use atomic weapons if necessary in the event of war, the British would be "accessories before the act" of any US action.

Eisenhower backed down on some of the British reservations for his speech, tactfully taking out references to the "obsolete colonial mold" in order to mollify Churchill. But on the wording over the US right to reserve the right to use atom bombs, there was no real change. Churchill was now satisfied, writing in a memorandum to the president that day, "I think it is a very fine speech. . . . It is a great pronouncement and will resound through the anxious and bewildered world."

But then the British and Americans had a private conversation over Korea, after the French had gone. The powerful differences between the two sides reemerged with vigor. Eisenhower and the US delegation wanted the United Kingdom to support "a vigorous offensive—using the atomic weapon against military objectives north of the Yalu river" if the new armistice were to be broken. Eisenhower and Dulles even went so far as to say that Moscow should be warned of the atomic option in such an event. But Churchill and Eden demurred—this time the two of them were in agreement. It was, they reminded the US delegates, a United Nations–brokered peace, not an American one.

Now both Eden and Churchill felt the profound concern of the effects on the United Kingdom if an atomic war broke out. What would happen, for example, in relation to the considerable number of American bombers with atomic weapons in the east of England. To this Eisenhower could only promise consultation.

Once more, Eisenhower's diary for December 8 is not in the main published edition, but does exist in the presidential archives in Abilene and has been quoted by historians. Churchill, he noted, had been in Bermuda a "curious mixture of belligerence and caution, sometimes amounting almost to hysterical fear." Eisenhower continued:

When he really wants to do something, he pooh-poohs and belittles every word or hint of risks involved. On the other hand, if he is in opposition to an argument—as for example the thought that we could count on using the atomic bomb to repel massive aggression in

Korea—he can rake up and expand upon every possible adverse effect on Russian intentions and reaction, and on public opinion throughout the world.

It is not surprising that Dulles's defense of the American New Look defense program to the Council of Foreign Relations on January 12, 1954, ended up having the opposite effect from the one intended, not so much scaring the Soviet Union and China, but as Kevin Ruane has so aptly put it, "badly spooking America's allies. The British, post-Bermuda, were edgier than most."

11

Churchill's Epiphany Moment

Churchill came back from Bermuda depressed as to what he could now do, since it seemed that the president was not interested in the Great Power conference of which the prime minister dreamed.

But on February 18, 1954, sitting in his bed in 10 Downing Street, he had what we could call an epiphany moment—he now discovered the truly devastating power of the new nuclear weapon in a way he had not really been able to do before. And it changed his life and the last months of his premiership, as well as the course of the war in Vietnam. For to Churchill and his British Cabinet colleagues, the two seemingly disparate issues were to become enmeshed, with the profoundest of consequences.

Churchill had the custom of reading the newspapers over breakfast in bed. February 18 was no exception. But *what* he read was an account in the *Manchester Guardian* of a speech given the previous day in Chicago by Sterling Cole, the chairman of the US Joint Congressional Committee on Atomic Energy. This described in awesome vividness the success of the American hydrogen bomb test, one that literally wiped out an entire island.

As Graham Farmelo describes, "Jock Colville walked into the room to find an agitated Churchill with his copy of the newspaper open on his bedside table. The prime minister's halitotic poodle was probably, as usual, yapping at the foot of the bed, his budgerigar chirruping in his cage or flying around the room."

Churchill proceeded to read an extract from the article to Colville: "[T]he heat and the blast generated . . . would cause absolute destruction over an area extending three miles in all directions. . . . The area of severe-to-moderate damage would stretch in all directions to several miles . . . the Russians would be able to deliver [such an attack on the United States] in 'one or two years from now.'"

Colville then observed that Churchill, "with a mix of triumph and indignation," called Eden, the secretary to the Cabinet, and each of the three Chiefs of Staff, to see if they knew such details themselves. All apparently did not, causing Churchill to retort to his private secretary, "It was lucky that at least one person in Whitehall read the newspapers."

For as the prime minister realized, this meant that Britain was now in the direct line of fire, since while the Soviets might not yet be able to reach the United States, they could certainly reach Britain and reduce its cities to rubble.

But Sterling Cole had been describing the 1952 test—"Mike." On March 1, 1954, the Americans exploded a massively more powerful hydrogen bomb on the Bikini Atoll, code-named Bravo. If anything, this was too successful—fifteen million tons of TNT, apparently three times greater than expected. Bravo destroyed several of the Marshall Islands, where the test took place, with the island of Eleugalab ceasing to exist. In addition, and unforeseen, the radioactive cloud that the blast created contaminated not just hundreds of unsuspecting Marshall Islanders, but a Japanese fishing boat around eighty miles away, whose name was translated as *Lucky Dragon No. 5*. The radiation eventually killed one of the crew and seriously injured the others.

This last misfortune could not be covered up, especially since the Japanese had been acutely conscious of radiation since Hiroshima and Nagasaki nine years earlier. As a consequence, the fate of the fishermen became global news and created a considerable international atmosphere of fear.

For Churchill there was another course of concern. Would the Americans use nuclear weapons as a last resort in the event of war?

A warm letter of Eisenhower's of February 9 was now seen in a context perhaps different from the one that the president had intended. Eisenhower had been hoping that the leading free nations of the world could come together in common cause to improve global security. Such a group would "rest solidly upon a common understanding of the Russian menace and in the clear conviction that only through unity, stubbornly maintained in the face of every inconsequential point of argument and difference between us, can these great things be achieved."

So far so good—this was essentially about deterrence. And as we shall see later, Eisenhower was already contemplating a group of nations in or connected with Southeast Asia/Indochina to deter possible Chinese aggression and deal with the Vietnam conflict.

But it was as Eisenhower waxed lyrically about the defense of civilization against the Communist menace that his wording began to cause alarm. His penultimate paragraph, pondering on the "Russian threat," went on to say:

It is only when one allows his mind to contemplate momentarily such a disaster for the world and attempts to picture an atheistic material-ism in complete domination of all human life, that he fully appreciates how necessary it is to seek renewed faith and strength from his God, and sharpen his sword for the struggle that cannot possibly be escaped.

Exactly what was implied in *the struggle that cannot possibly be escaped?* It was this phrase that seriously worried Anthony Eden, who told Churchill on March 2 that he found "it very difficult to assess the real meaning of Ike's message." If the president were merely "thinking aloud" (as a literal meaning of the letter would suggest), then Eden is right to say there was no problem.

But, Eden went on to say, what exactly did "sharpen his sword" for an inescapable struggle actually mean? One hideous interpretation was possible:

Taken by themselves, the words could mean that the president thinks that a war with the Soviet Union cannot be escaped and that we should build up our armaments with that end in view.

If Eisenhower meant a spiritual struggle, that was fine, but Churchill should make sure that the president was not speaking of the inevitability of *war*, as surely neither Britain nor the United States would want that outcome.

The prime minister, as we read in Graham Farmelo's wonderful account, *Churchill's Bomb,* had spoken to his scientists, so when he replied to Eisenhower on March 8, he had all the important facts at his fingertips. Having given the experts' reaction to the nuclear tests, he went on to tell the president the truth:

You can imagine what my thoughts are about London. I am told that several million people would certainly be obliterated by four or five of the latest H bombs. In a few more years these could be delivered by rocket. . . . New York and your other great cities have immeasurable perils too.

Churchill fully understood that with such weapons, talk of "superiority" in weapons "loses much of its meaning." And he prophesied the reality of *mutually assured destruction*, the dangers of which he was well ahead of his time in predicting.

And the speech by Sterling Cole was still seared into his consciousness. Seldom has the case of thoughtless nuclear buildup while ignoring its perils been better made than by what Churchill now went on to tell the president:

> *When I read Mr. Cole's widely reported speech, I was so surprised that its searing statements attracted so little comment. The reason is that human minds recoil from the realization of such facts. The people, including the well-informed, can only gape and console themselves with the reflection that death comes to all anyhow, sometime. This merciful numbness cannot be enjoyed by the few men upon whom the supreme responsibility falls.*

Biographers of Churchill who claim that he now wanted to stay on as prime minister for genuine, *bona fide* reasons, and not retire in 1954 as Eden and others in the Cabinet so devoutly wished, are vindicated by what he said next:

> *All the things that are happening now put together, added to all the material things that have ever happened, are scarcely more important to the human race. I consider that you and, if my strength last, I cannot flinch from the mental exertions involved.*

War, he concluded, was not inevitable, and it was vital now to have a settlement of the kind for which he had yearned.

12

Butter Not Bombs

On May 7, 1954, news reached the West that Dien Bien Phu had finally fallen to the Viet Minh. Eisenhower and his administration now began negotiating with the French government for the United States formally to join the war—they would respond to a French invitation to do so.

But on June 18, the situation drastically changed. Pierre Mendès France, the French Radical politician, became the new prime minister. There would be no invitation to the United States to enter a war. Instead, he wanted peace—as in fact did the vast majority of his fellow citizens, for whom the continuing war and its death rate was becoming inacceptable.

There was also now a recess in the Geneva talks, which meant that Eden was able to accompany Churchill to the United States on June 25, for what would be the great man's last formal talks in Washington. To wise ministers such as Harold Macmillan, Eden's presence at Churchill's side was a relief.

While Eisenhower's press secretary, James Hegarty, might have dismissed Churchill as being "almost in his dotage," the shock the prime minister had received when he read about the effects of the new hydrogen bomb in the *Manchester Guardian* four months earlier showed that on the key issue of the day, his mind remained focused as ever. The awesome power of the new weapon, Churchill told his American hosts, "transformed what had been to him a vague scientific nightmare into something which dominates the whole world." War with an atomic bomb—the kind used at Hiroshima—could have been feasible. But he had now come to understand that the "H-bomb is something totally different." And with the devastation of earlier wars in mind, he realized that the old kind of bomb shelters would be "useless in a thermonuclear attack." (American readers of a certain age will remember the school drills in which everyone had to hide under their desk in the event of a nuclear attack. That might have helped protect them if the ceiling fell on their head, but the radiation would have killed them all instantly!)

When Eisenhower pointed out the massive superiority of the American stock of such weapons over the Soviets, Churchill responded that "the safety of the world depended on this deterrent—on the capacity for an overwhelming retort."

However, the talks now moved in a very positive direction. Eisenhower was fine about British plans to build an independent nuclear deterrent. With the McMahon Act close to repeal, he was able to give a considerable amount of technical information to the British delegation. As Eisenhower had already realized, it was important to grant Churchill's wish that American nuclear weapons be refitted so that they could be transported by Royal Air Force planes, an undertaking the United States was to implement swiftly. And on August 30 the Atomic Energy Act would be put into law, allowing considerably greater leeway for the United States to share secrets with close allies than had been the case hitherto.

This was all good news—Churchill had reason to be pleased. But in thinking that Eisenhower would give active approval to the dream of a Big Three summit of the kind that had taken place at Tehran, Yalta, or Potsdam, the prime minister alas deluded himself. And to be fair to him, others equally misinterpreted American *bonhomie*. Colville recorded:

> *W at once got down talking to the president. The first and vast surprise was when the latter at once agreed to talks with the Russians—a possibility of which W had hoped to persuade the Americans after long talks on Indo-China, Europe, atoms; on all of these first impressions were surprisingly and immediately satisfactory while the world believes in general that there is at this moment greater Anglo-American friction than ever in history and that these talks are fraught with every possible complication and difficulty.*

So it is easy to see how Churchill had, as Kevin Ruane puts it, got ahead of himself. Unfortunately this optimism was misplaced. As Colville observed two days into the talks, the "Russian project"—the Three Power summit—"has shrunk again as Dulles has been getting at the president. W still determined to meet the Russians as he now has an assurance that the Americans won't object." Sadly, Churchill was wrong.

And just when all had gone so well in Washington, DC, Churchill now took action that created a crisis in Anglo-American relations all over again. On his way back from the United States by boat, Churchill confessed to his physician, Lord Moran:

I am counting on the Russians wanting a better time; they want butter, not bombs, more comfort. For forty years they have had a pretty tough life. They may have given up dreams of world conquest and be ready for peaceful co-existence. Anyway, Ike has crossed the gulf which separates a mission to destroy Bolshevism from living side by side in peace. I must admit that I myself have crossed that gulf. I would like to visit Russia once more before I die.

In reality, not until Harold Macmillan's visit to Moscow in 1959 did a British prime minister visit the Soviet capital, and then in the very different era of Nikita Khrushchev as leader of the USSR. And Churchill's policy, while in many ways *idealist* in terms of wanting a solution to the existential problem of nuclear war, was also *realist* in how he perceived the Soviets and their intentions—butter not bombs. It forgets, in a way that the founding fathers of containment in the United States, such as George Kennan, had not, that the Soviet Union was by definition an *ideological* state.

It might not be able to send tanks over the Iron Curtain on a campaign of conquest—there Churchill was right—but Soviet leadership still believed in *Communism*, and that political ideology was as strong as it had ever been. However scary Dulles might seem with his Cold War warrior rhetoric—and by 1954 he was frightening the daylights out of millions of people around the world, including in the British Cabinet—he was right in his ideological perception of the USSR. The Soviet leaders really were Communists. And we should expect them to be—that is the belief system for which they had devoted their lives, and to which they still adhered despite the horrors of the Stalin era. It is surely cynical to suppose—as realists do—that people wear their faith lightly. On the contrary, the whole of human history has shown what millions will do in the name of religion or patriotism or, as in the case of the Soviets, political dogma. So butter, yes, but Bolshevism, too.

Furthermore, Churchill had completely misunderstood Eisenhower, to what would prove to be harmful results. "I am planning to go to meet the Russians, if they would like it," he told Moran. And then he showed what a misinterpretation of the president he had made:

> *Ike has crossed a gulf of thought. . . . He has made up his mind that Communism is not something that we must at all costs wipe out, but rather something we have got to learn to live with, and alongside— peaceful coexistence.*

In one sense this was right. Contrary to the fears of many in Britain, Eisenhower was not some crazed general out of a later film such as *Dr Strangelove*. There were no plans simply to invade the Soviet bloc just for Cold War reasons. The president was no reckless ideologue. But he did have the firm view that caving in too easily to the Soviets, without firm proof of their intentions, was deeply unwise, as the correspondence between him and Churchill would now go on to reveal. Eisenhower wanted peace, too, but he had not given his British colleague *carte blanche* to go to Moscow and just start talking.

As he told one of his aides, "Winston has a wonderful way of turning conversations at some later time into ironclad agreements . . . . We surely want to avoid that."

In essence, who was right? Was it Eisenhower and Dulles and the Cold War prism through which they perceived everything? Or was it Churchill in his dreams of making the world a safer place?

After the First World War, a British satirical history book was written, titled *1066 and All That*, which because of its humor remains in print a century later. In their description of the Civil War in the seventeenth century, the authors famously described Oliver Cromwell and the Roundheads as "right but repulsive" and King Charles I and the Cavaliers as "wrong but wromantic [*sic*]," phrases that have gone down in British popular folklore ever since.

Can one describe the clash in perceptions between Churchill and the Americans in similar terms? Was Churchill being "wrong but wromantic" in his dreams? Was Dulles, the slab-faced Washington ideologue, in some sense "right but repulsive"?

One historian, who has brought refreshing new light on the whole issue of Churchill, nuclear war, and the quest for peace, has written:

The prime minister's visit to North America [in June 1954] is noteworthy for another reason rarely if ever mentioned in the literature. It was now, for the first time in the Cold War, that Churchill comprehended that détente and its corollary, the reduction of the danger of nuclear war, were unattainable unless the Western powers took seriously the Kremlin's calls (dating from the time of Stalin's death) for peaceful coexistence.

Churchill had made this clear in his reaction to journalists he met in Canada between his trip to Washington, DC, and his ship journey home. He denied vehemently the very notion that he was in any way appeasing the USSR. "We have to live with all sorts of people in this wicked world," and the two great world ideologies, capitalism and communism, should now learn to coexist "side by side."

As Kevin Ruane aptly comments, for "a man who had made a career of demonizing communism, this was quite a statement."

That is surely correct—although it is also accurate to say, as we saw earlier in this book, that the anti-Bolshevik Churchill had, in 1941, welcomed the USSR as an ally in the fight against Hitler, swallowed decades of rhetoric, and embraced Stalin as an ally. In 1941 Nazism was the existential threat, and now it was the possibility that Britain could be annihilated in a nuclear war. One could therefore argue that for Churchill national survival eclipsed ideology, and this once more proved to be the case. As he put it to the Press Club luncheon in Washington, DC, on June 28:

I am not anti-Russian; I am violently anti-Communist, but I do beg you to make sure that no stone is left unturned in this period to give them a chance to grasp the prospects of great material well-being . . . and I am rather inclined to think, if I had to make a prediction, that they will not throw away such an opportunity.

In 1945 Churchill had informed his colleagues that he could deal with Stalin. The events of the next few years proved that this was a rather optimistic view. The Soviet Union kept hold of Central and South-East Europe, and freedom was extinguished. The Soviet extinction of Hungarian liberty in 1956 would prove that even if Stalin's excesses had been denounced and large-scale purges made a thing of the past, Communist ideology did not permit dissent.

But was Churchill wrong but nonetheless "wromantic" in his aspirations? Perhaps. Historians also argue that up until now, Churchill had also hoped that the United States, with its strategic nuclear superiority, would one day be able to "roll back" (to use the American phrase) the post-Yalta frontiers and liberate those under the Soviet yoke—and most certainly prevent a Soviet invasion of democratic Europe and an extension westward of Moscow's power. However, in the light of the nuclear bomb and the brand-new set of circumstances, to quote Kevin Ruane again, at "no point between 1945 and 1954 did he ever concede that Eastern Europe was lost. Now he did."

Not until 1989 were the peoples of Central and Eastern Europe liberated from their oppressors, and then, so wonderfully, without any of the nuclear conflagration that Churchill understandably so feared. Although not all the countries of the old Soviet bloc are paragons of liberal democracy in the 2020s, the epochal events of that glorious year resound still.

But in 1954 that wonderful new dawn was thirty-five years into a future that could not possibly be seen. Things would get worse—the Berlin Wall, the crushing of the Prague Spring by Warsaw Pact forces in 1968, the suppression of Solidarity in Poland in 1981—all these made life for millions of people living in what has rightly been described as the common European home, unbearable for decades. If even the *Economist* in early 1989 could not predict the fall of the Iron Curtain, how could anyone have foretold back in the 1950s how the rest of the century would turn out.

Churchill, with his firm grasp of the horrors of nuclear war, surely had a case in wanting to go and see Molotov and make one last effort for détente. But the acceptance of the Iron Curtain, its inevitability and permanence, came at a price, paid by millions of Poles, Hungarians, and

Czechs, most of whom would never live to see freedom regained. In hoping for rollback until 1954, the undoing of Yalta, the dismantling of the division of Europe that had so sorrowed Churchill in his speech at Fulton in 1946, he had, one could say, been pursuing a chimera. Rollback would have led to war, and possible use of atomic bombs. But the hope of restoring freedom, however hopeless, was surely an honorable one, and now, in the interests of détente, it had to be abandoned.

Now on board ship, en route home to England, Churchill was to demonstrate that his misunderstanding of Eisenhower was not simply a mistake but also potentially dangerous. He consequently embarked on a piece of unilateral foreign policy making that, as we shall see, nearly cost him his premiership. Thankfully, the diaries of Jock Colville (who was on board with him) and Harold Macmillan (who found things out and recorded them for posterity) give us fascinating insights on what now took place. Macmillan's account ties in with Colville's, and as Macmillan was a major political player, we can follow his account and see what Colville's diaries add.

Once safely at sea, away from the Americans and the British Embassy and not yet subject to the pressure of the London Cabinet and the Foreign Office, Churchill decided to act. He drafted the Molotov telegram—in rather more unsuitable and sentimental terms than the form that ultimately went, but substantially the same.

Needless to say, his staff insisted that he show it to Eden, who was, after all, the foreign secretary. According to Colville, whose interpretation is surely correct, Eden had come by boat with the others rather than the quicker route of flying back by plane, in order to plead his case with Churchill to speed up matters and allow Eden to succeed him as prime minister that year—previous intrigues had suggested a date in September. This in effect meant that Eden's ambitions clashed with his policy objections, since he obviously did not want to do anything to harm his chances of becoming prime minister within just a few months. This is the essential context for the events that now unfolded.

(On another occasion, Macmillan, perhaps cruelly but hideously accurate, said of Eden that he had been trained to win the great horse race the Derby in 1938, but was not let out of the stalls until 1955. Macmillan, remembering vividly how Eden had pulled his punches over Munich in 1938—leaving the powerful opposition to Chamberlain's betrayal of the Czechs to Churchill—knew that the foreign secretary utterly lacked the killer instinct, as the discussions in 1954 now proved.)

Eden, with good cause, "objected in the strongest terms" to Churchill's Molotov initiative. Macmillan now discovered what had happened on the boat.

> *They wrangled for hours. For one whole day they refused to meet. All the communication was by written minute, from one "suite" on the boat to another. . . . At last, under the pressure of the tremendous force of this old man's [i.e., Churchill's] character, Eden gave way—at least to this extent.*

Macmillan knew Eden's character as well: "He did not say 'I will resign if you send that telegram, it will be contrary to the advice of your foreign secretary.' That was enough for Churchill."

So there was a compromise—a draft would be sent to RA Butler (referred to by everyone by his initials: RAB), chancellor of the exchequer and the Cabinet minister in charge in London while Churchill and Eden were both away. Eden presumed that Butler would show it to other members of the Cabinet, which, given their likely reaction, would result in the whole process being delayed. But this was a mistake—Butler made a few amendments and sent the annotated version back to Churchill on the boat, without anyone else seeing it.

Macmillan was right to presume that Butler would have presupposed that Eisenhower had agreed to the initiative during the talks in Washington, which of course was not at all the case. The telegram was therefore sent with Butler's cuts accepted—as Macmillan said, essentially no different from the original.

Macmillan summarized Eden's weakness in devastating fashion:

> *Eden made two serious errors. He ought to have said 'I will resign if you send that telegram', or—'I will resign if you send that telegram without informing and securing the consent of the Cabinet' or 'I will*

resign if you send that telegram without at least informing the President'. But he allowed P.M to overwhelm him.

And Macmillan was aware, too, of how Churchill felt:

He was absolutely determined; nothing would shake him; he would go on alone; if his colleagues abandoned him, he would appeal to the country, who would support him. All this from strength. It was his last passionate wish—an old man's dream—an old man's folly, perhaps, but it might save the world.

Was it "folly" on Churchill's part—*wrong but wromantic?* Or perhaps wromantic but unrealistic—would the Soviets really agree to such talks without the Americans being present? The debate now switched from the boat to those Cabinet colleagues whom Churchill had so carefully ignored, with Macmillan and Salisbury given advance notice, making them, as Macmillan noticed, accessories after the fact to the prime minister's actions, along with Eden and Butler.

This is what Churchill wrote to Molotov (with those passages erased by Butler in roman and thus not in the final edition):

I wonder how my American expedition has reacted on what you feel about the wish I expressed on May 11, 1953 for a top level meeting of the Big Three, and upon the statements I have made from time to time in the House of Commons, that if that were impossible I would seek to make contact myself with your Government if that were desired by them. It is clear to me that at the present time the United States would not participate, but you have no doubt read the very much more favourable statement by President Eisenhower in his Press Conference of June 30. Her Majesty's Government do not of course have to obtain permission from anyone in such matters. *My feeling is that the United States would make it as good for me with their public opinion as they should.*

This was extraordinary, with or without the excision by Butler. It is clear that Churchill was going off on his own, and was presuming a great deal of American goodwill for his proposed bilateral adventure.

He then confessed he had written the telegram before consulting his own Cabinet (again Butler removed the words that revealed Churchill's action):

> *The question is: how would your Government feel about it? I would like to know before I ask the Cabinet we make you an official proposal. Anthony Eden, with whom you have had so many friendly talks, would of course come with me.*

Churchill would naturally wish to meet Malenkov, who the British government perceived—wrongly as it turned out—was the true leader of the USSR.

And it is easy to see why the Americans would be so worried when Churchill went on to add:

> *I should be very glad if you let me know if they [the Soviet leadership] like the idea of a friendly meeting, with no object and no agenda and no object but to find a reasonable way of living side by side in growing confidence, easement and prosperity . . . [that] might be the prelude to a larger reunion where much might be settled. I have, however, no warrant to say this beyond my own hopes.*

An abbreviated version of the above was sent to Eisenhower.

"No warrant"! How true that was! This was indeed the butter not bombs approach he had suggested to Lord Moran a few days before. But it was very much Churchill's private initiative.

Churchill returned to London on July 6, 1954. And now he unwittingly launched himself into a grave political crisis, what his ever acute and thoughtful Cabinet colleague Harold Macmillan rightly called a "bombshell."

For on July 7 the prime minister informed his astonished Cabinet of the telegram he had sent on board ship to Molotov—to go to Moscow for talks. It did not take long for the astute around that table in 10 Downing Street to realize he had done so without any consultation with Eisenhower, and as a unilateral act of prime ministerial power since most of the Cabinet had not been consulted either.

His words on the voyage to Colville were now proved to be prescient. He had confided in him that he would make talks with the Soviets "a matter of confidence with the Cabinet.... . If they opposed the visit, it would give him a good occasion to go." So sending it *before* docking in Southampton was part of a game plan devised by Churchill. As Colville recalled later, "[I]f he had waited to consult the Cabinet after the *Queen Elizabeth* returned, they would almost certainly have raised objections and caused delays."

Not only that, Colville remembered:

> *The stakes in this matter were so high and, as he sees it, the possible benefits so crucial to our survival, that he was prepared to adopt any methods to getting a meeting with the Russians arranged.*

In other words, he was going to bounce them into agreeing with his *fait accompli*.

In addition, the other problem was that most of them had also not been informed of the other decision that Churchill now proposed to spring upon them—that Britain was now a nuclear power in the process of manufacturing its own hydrogen bomb. Two key issues—the telegram to Moscow, and Britain being an independent nuclear power—were now effectively conflated, in a way that was rapidly to prove both divisive and contentious. This uniting of the two was, as Kevin Ruane rightly reminds us, all "because of the politically toxic convergence of Churchill's bomb-making and his peace-making," which, one could add, were his fault, since had he dealt with them sequentially, the crisis that now erupted need never have taken place.

The Cabinet meeting on July 7 was therefore to prove merely the start of a tumultuous set of meetings, which showed that the politicians around the table were nowhere near as compliant as Churchill had foolishly presumed. Objections and delays would now come thick and fast, not just because of disagreement on the issues themselves but *constitutionally*—this was not the way in which a prime minister, even someone as august as Winston Churchill, should ever be able to treat his colleagues.

Theoretically speaking, a British prime minister is *primus inter pares*—Latin for "first among equals"—since it is the Queen who is the head of state, not the prime minister, and therefore is quite unlike the situation in the United States where the president is both the elected head of state and thus the nation's chief executive, and the Cabinet exists at the president's command, even if their appointments have to be ratified by the Senate. Churchill and Eisenhower were, relatively speaking, in very different political positions. What follows shows that clearly, and demonstrates that even Winston Churchill—surely now the embodiment of an old man in a hurry—could have brought down his own government.

Churchill's scientific guru, Frederick Lindemann (Lord Cherwell), was brought into the meeting to enunciate the reasons why it was a good idea for the United Kingdom to be part of the hydrogen bomb club. It was important as a deterrent for Britain's safety—those contemplating an attack on the country would naturally be deterred if the British were able to retaliate in their own right with their own bombs. And of course there was the factor of prestige; the idea still held decades later that possession of this weapon gave Britain a place at the top table.

Churchill told the Cabinet what has in effect been British policy on such matters ever since, that "we could not expect to maintain our influence as a world Power unless we possessed the most up-to-date nuclear weapons. The prime aim of our policy was to prevent major war; and the possession of these weapons was now the main deterrent to a potential aggressor."

This has been the case for nuclear deterrent from that time to the present: The point of having nuclear weapons is that their deterrent value *means they never have to be used.* In that, over sixty years after Churchill shared this with his colleagues, his view has been vindicated. World War III has not taken place.

Churchill's secretive actions caused the displeasure of ordinary members of the Cabinet at being hitherto excluded from *both* decisions—the Molotov telegram and the decision for an independent nuclear deterrent—now fused into anger and resentment at the deception and oversight, and they now vocally voiced their anger. It was, as Macmillan, who *had* been consulted ahead, said, "dramatic . . . a most extraordinary scene." The leader of the House of Commons "at once made a most vigorous protest at so momentous a decision being communicated to the Cabinet in so cavalier a way."

As Macmillan recalled a few days later, Churchill really had acted unilaterally in writing to the Soviets: "To my horror, I learned that the president knew nothing at all about this—altho' the P.M had been his guest only a few days before." At an impromptu meeting at the Foreign Office, Eden explained to Macmillan and Lord Salisbury the extraordinary events on the ship. Yet when Macmillan and Churchill spoke to each other, the prime minister insisted that Eisenhower was not at all "shocked" by these events—wrongly, as we shall soon see.

Macmillan put his private social network to good use when he contacted Sir Harold Caccia at the Foreign Office. The truth was now emerging! Eisenhower had known of Churchill's wishes for a summit, but had "treated it all rather lightly if not jocularly. He hates all these telegrams and visits from Churchill, and is acutely embarrassed by them."

The Cabinet broke up in disarray. Macmillan was horrified at the possibility of a split—it should not be forgotten that the government's majority in the House of Commons was slim, and that winning the next general election was not by any means a foregone conclusion. He therefore talked to Colville and told him that Churchill "must go at once, on the grounds of health, to avoid a disaster." When Colville complained, Macmillan replied, "I am devoted to Winston and admire him more than any man. But he is not fit. He cannot function. . . . He must take it seriously and realise how deeply he has hurt us."

The anger felt by Eisenhower on Churchill's presumption over the Molotov telegram is evident from the president's letter to the prime minister sent that very day. There could no longer be any ambiguity in Eisenhower's true feelings.

You did not let any grass grow under your feet. When you left here I had thought, obviously erroneously, that you were in an undecided mood about this matter, and that when you had cleared your own mind I would receive some notice if you were to put your program into action.

Eisenhower was briefly conciliatory, hoping that if he were similarly to say something, he would give Churchill notice of his own thoughts.

However, the president's position and that of the United States was plain: His recollection of the Washington meeting did not coincide with the prime minister's:

I shall probably say something to the effect that while you were here the possibility of a Big Three meeting was discussed; that I could not see how it would serve a useful purpose at this time; that you then suggested an exploratory mission of your own; that I said this would be essentially your own responsibility and decision. Finally, I said that if you did undertake such a mission, your plan would carry our hopes for the best but would not engage our responsibility.

Eisenhower also expounded on how Churchill could be misunderstood in the United States—and this was prescient since it very much concerned many members of Churchill's own Cabinet in the discussions that followed. Once more the president could not have put it more explicitly:

The fact that your message to Moscow was sent so promptly after you left here is likely to give an impression more powerful than your cautioning words that in some way your plan was agreed at our meeting. Of course, the dating of your message may not become public. This I think would be best because it will call for less explanation from me to the American public. In any event, I think you will agree that your program should be handled with the greatest delicacy to avoid giving either the misapprehension that we are in fact party to it, or the equally dangerous misapprehension that your action in this matter reflects a sharp disagreement between our two countries. I know that

you will be aware of these twin dangers and I hope that by under-
standing and cooperation we can surmount this.

Although Eisenhower had not said as much, it was evident that he indeed felt there *was* a "sharp disagreement" between, if not Britain and the United States, clearly himself and Churchill. And this is extraordinary, in light of the fact that the Anglo-American "special relationship" was supposed to be at the heart of Churchill's every breath, something agreed both by his historical defenders, for whom he is the icon and epitome of Anglosphere harmony and unity, and by the revisionists, who regard him as an outright appeaser of the United States who sold his country's birth-right to abase himself before America and all its wishes. Here, however, both sides are arguably wrong, since Churchill was now in effect putting his profound wish for nuclear peace *ahead of* the "special relationship."

So when the Cabinet resumed the next day, on July 8, their assent to Churchill's wishes was by no means a done deal. Even the very morality of the hydrogen bomb came into the discussion.

The slightly anodyne official Cabinet minutes cover up the depth of anger, and who said what. But even the account below shows that a genu-ine debate nonetheless took place. And the *real* reason for Britain having its own nuclear bomb is most revealing:

At present some people thought that the greatest risk was that the United States might plunge the world into war, either through a mis-judged intervention in Asia or to forestall an attack by Russia. Our best chance of preventing this was to maintain our influence with the United States Government and they would certainly feel more respect for our views if we continued to play an effective part in building up the strength necessary to deter aggression than if we left it entirely up to them to match and counter Russia's strength in thermo-nuclear weapons.

The importance of this cannot be exaggerated. The reason why Brit-ain needed to have its own nuclear weapons was because of the *American* danger to world peace. This surely puts the whole issue into a radically different perspective. In essence the rationale for the United Kingdom to possess its own deterrence was not just the danger of Britain being wiped out in a Soviet nuclear attack—although that of course remained the case—but to protect the country from a rogue *American* first use in Asia or Europe.

And this is why the "special relationship" was important—to give Britain a place at the top table *to keep the Americans under control.* This surely puts the relationship's reason for being in a different light from the one normally believed.

Such reasoning convinced most of the Cabinet, who now went along with the decision for the independent nuclear deterrent. But the sense of aggravation had not gone away, and it rose once more over the issue of Churchill's unilateral decision to visit Molotov in Moscow. Here his fellow ministers were determined to be less amenable.

Macmillan was impressed with his old wartime colleague Eisenhower's reply to Churchill, calling it "a fine answer—generous and noble." All now depended on how Eisenhower replied to Churchill's reply of *mea culpa.* "The Cabinet," Macmillan recalled, "were very quiet but rather grim. . . . Eden said nothing."

The July 8 Cabinet meeting was not held at 10 Downing Street but in Churchill's room in the House of Commons. Macmillan described it as "the most dramatic . . . which I have attended." This was because discussion was not so much over the substance of the Molotov telegram but the way in which the Cabinet felt it had been treated.

And as Macmillan realized, Eden had been there before. Churchill's rationale was that as prime minister he had every right to correspond with whomever he wished. But it was Neville Chamberlain's decision to correspond behind Eden's back with the Italian dictator Mussolini that had been the last straw for Eden as foreign secretary in 1938—the reason he resigned. *That* resignation would be turned into legend by Churchill in his work *The Gathering Storm,* with Eden as the brave and principled anti-appeaser resigning and standing against Chamberlain and appeasement. Now Eden was in the same position again, with a prime minister conducting his own foreign policy without the foreign secretary's express support.

It was, now in 1954, Lord Salisbury, who as Lord Cranborne had resigned from the Foreign Office in 1938 in solidarity with Eden, who led the charge against Churchill's private foreign policy. As he described the prime minister's actions: "Two days at sea, he had left the president uninformed. Two days from home, he had kept his colleagues in the dark." In the minutes of the meeting record, Salisbury also made the deadly but accurate point: "Was the message so urgent that its despatch could not have been delayed for three days?" And suppose, he argued, the Cabinet rejected the prime minister's personal diplomacy and deemed the telegram a mistake? As Churchill had *already* sent Molotov the message, the Soviets could well expose the prime minister's telegram to the public if the Cabinet were to reject it—and the split between Churchill and his Cabinet would thus be revealed.

Salisbury threatened to resign, and Macmillan observed:

Churchill was very much moved. At one moment his face went dead white—at the next it was puce. I really thought he was going to have another stroke. As Salisbury spoke, there was a tense, dramatic silence.

Later that day Eden asked Macmillan to visit him at the Foreign Office. The former was "obviously very worried. Churchill has begun to let him down again. He knows, in his heart, that he ought to have resigned on the boat."

This shows not just Eden's weakness but also Churchill's strength. Had Eden resigned, it would inevitably have sunk his chances of succeeding Churchill as prime minister. In 1938 he had resigned, but in pulling his punches rather than going all out to attack Chamberlain, he in effect ensured that it was Churchill—the hitherto despised reactionary who had spent the 1930s in political exile on the back benches—who was given a key post in the War Cabinet in 1939 and was thus in the right position to succeed Chamberlain in 1940. Eden had thrown away his chances, and now, by his dithering, was endangering his future yet again.

Churchill, at the urging of his colleagues, now wrote a semi-contrite message back to Eisenhower. It is a wonderful understatement:

*I hope you are not vexed with me for not submitting to you the
text of my telegram to Molotov [before it was sent]. I felt that as it
was a private and personal enquiry which I had not brought offi-
cially before the Cabinet I had better bear the burden myself and
not involve you in any way. I thought this would be agreeable to
you, and that we could then consider the question in the light of the
answer I got.*

Disingenuous? Is this a naughty schoolchild being discovered up to
mischief by a teacher? Churchill then expounded the view he had often
expressed since Stalin's death: that conditions in the USSR had now
changed, and that the new regime would be open to talks. And just to
make it plain, he admitted:

*It is on all this that I most earnestly seek your advice, while being will-
ing to bear the brunt of failure on my own shoulders. . . . Meanwhile
we shall keep you most thoroughly informed and I shall not seek any
decision to make an official approach until I hear from you again. . . .
There can be no question of a public announcement before our two
governments have consulted together about policy and have agreed on
what it is best to say.*

This was a double climb down by Churchill—not just to Eisenhower
but also to his irate government colleagues still stinging at being excluded
from so vital a policy decision.

Most of Eisenhower's reply on July 8 was in fact about the war in
Indochina, and his concern that the United Kingdom would formally
admit the People's Republic of China to the United Nations, which, significantly, was to the president a moral issue, one of justice and principle.
(Britain had recognized the PRC as the lawful government of China in
1950, something the Americans refused to do until Nixon's famous visit
quite some years later.)

On the substantive issue of Molotov and Churchill's solitary diplomacy, Eisenhower was much more emollient.

Of course I am not vexed. Personal trust based on more than a dozen years of close association and valued friendship may occasionally permit room for amazement but never for suspicion. Moreover, I cannot too strongly emphasize to you my prayerful hope that your mission, if you pursue it, may be crowned with complete success. My appreciation of the acute need for peace and understanding in the world certainly far transcends any personal pride in my judgments and convictions. No one could be happier than I to find that I have been wrong in my conclusion that the men in the Kremlin are not to be trusted, however great the apparent solemnity and sincerity with which they might enter into an agreement or engagement. . . . Frankly, I have no worries whatsoever about the ability of your Government and this one to keep Anglo-American relationships on a sound friendly and cooperative basis.

The one caveat was the admission of China to the United Nations.

Churchill now began a gentle retreat. On July 9 he shared with the Cabinet both Eisenhower's telegram and his own proposed reply. He essentially ignored the American concern over China—a point noted by Macmillan in his diary—and suggested that the key issue was to "press for a more definitive expression of the president's views on some of the practical aspects of his [Churchill's] proposal for a meeting with M. Malenkov." The prime minister had now agreed that the meeting should be in a neutral venue—ideally in Bern after the Geneva Conference was over. As proof of Soviet sincerity, the USSR should be asked, for example, to ratify the Austrian treaty (which the Soviet Union did in 1955, the only time that they ever gave up territory when they withdrew their occupation troops from Austria).

Once again Lord Salisbury threatened to resign. And the Cabinet now decided to postpone the visit yet further—nothing should happen until the Geneva Conference on Vietnam was over. This seemed to prove a face-saver for everyone involved, so all decisions were thus put firmly on hold. As Churchill confessed in his telegram to Eisenhower, which summarized all these discussions:

Of course all this may be moonshine. The Soviets might refuse any meeting place but Moscow. In that case all would be off for the present. Or they [the USSR] will give nothing and merely seek, quite vainly, to split Anglo-American unity. I cherish hopes not illusions and after all I am "expendable" and very ready to be one in so great a cause.

Churchill returned to this theme in a speech to the House of Commons in a debate on July 12, in which he gave his hopes, and also carefully omitted any reference to the heated debate in his own Cabinet over the Molotov telegram. In his concluding remarks he told the assembled members of Parliament:

I have a final thought, which I do not think will raise disagreement, to present to this House, and I should be glad for it to travel as far as my words can reach. . . . [Eden had used the words "peaceful coexistence."] This fundamental and far-reaching conception certainly had its part in some of our conversations in Washington, and I was very glad when I read, after we had left, that President Eisenhower had said that the hope of the world lies in peaceful co-existence of the Communist and non-Communist Powers, adding also the warning, with which I entirely agree, that this doctrine must not lead to appeasement that compels nations to submit to foreign domination.

Churchill was thus being careful to stress that in his own wishes for peaceful coexistence with the Soviet Union, he was not guilty in the way that Neville Chamberlain had been back in the 1930s. But how the "easement" that Churchill wanted in Soviet-Western relationships and the appeasement of the pre-war years were different is never explicitly spelled out—and there were plenty of hard-liners in the United States who argued at the time that the two were essentially the same.

In winding up, he returned to two key themes—that of the English-speaking peoples and that of the threat of nuclear annihilation. And as has been clear in this chapter, there was a danger, to which he did not refer, of a clash between his two primary issues of concern. For it is evident that the Americans perceived the hydrogen bomb differently, as a legitimate weapon in the arsenal should war escalate to the extent that it became necessary to use it to counteract the tactical superiority of Warsaw Pact ground forces.

Toward the end of the debate, Churchill suggested:

The House must not under-rate the importance of this broad measure of concurrence of what in this case I may call the English-speaking world. What a vast ideological gulf there is between the idea of peaceful coexistence vigilantly safeguarded, and the mood of forcibly extirpating the Communist fallacy and heresy.

So Communism was wrong—but war, he reminded his listeners, would be far worse:

This statement is a recognition of the appalling character which war has now assumed and that its fearful consequences go even beyond the difficulties and dangers of dwelling side by side with Communist States.

This was not appeasement, therefore—though he did not expound this as such, but as simple recognition of the new and utterly different world that nuclear weapons had created.

He concluded in recognition of the realities—and of the way in which they would have an impact for some time to come:

Indeed, I believe that the widespread acceptance of this policy [i.e., peaceful coexistence] may in the passage of years ahead lead to the problems which divide the world being solved or solving themselves, as so many problems do, in a manner which will avert the mass destruction of the human race and give time, human nature and the mercy of God their chance to win salvation for us.

Most of Eisenhower's missive to Churchill on July 13 was again about the possibility of British support for the admission of the People's Republic—what the president referred to as "Red China"—into the

United Nations. Here the situation in Congress was now calmer and the hard-liners no longer as anti-British as had recently been the case.

On the Molotov issue Eisenhower was again emollient, not forbidding it but unable to promise that the "United States public" would regard it benignly, perhaps seeing it in the same way as Prohibition, what Hoover had once described as a "noble experiment." But Churchill would have to meet the Soviets on the "basis of full equality," and "Russian deeds are necessary as well as words."

This was hardly a ringing endorsement, but Churchill presented it as such to the Cabinet meeting the same day. But all decisions were to be postponed until Eden returned from the Geneva Conference.

On July 20 the conference succeeded, with Vietnam being divided at the 17th Parallel. Although we now know this was only a lull before a much greater war, at the time it was deemed to be a massive international success, with eight years of war brought to a close. Eden, who was rightly given the credit for the triumph, noted that "we had . . . reduced international tension at a point of instant danger to world peace. This achievement was well worth while."

The internal political crisis in Britain, however, was not yet over. Eisenhower had written a massive "Eyes Only" dispatch to Churchill on July 22 in which the president gave his views in some detail. (We saw extracts from this exchange in the Introduction—this is now the historical context.)

Eisenhower understood that Churchill was contemplating retirement to enable Eden to have enough time in Downing Street before a general election. And, he realized, it was therefore the prime minister's wish to achieve something major for the cause of peace, an aspiration with which the president empathized. But then came the strong note of caution:

I must also say that because of my utter lack of confidence in the reliability and integrity of the men in the Kremlin and my feeling that you may be disappointed in your present hopes, my mind has been turning toward an exploration of other possibilities by which you would still give to the world something inspiring before you laid down your official responsibilities.

In his solution Eisenhower suggested something that today would make enormous sense, and which puts him firmly on the side of the modern world that he so wished to be created. The best way to save what would later be described as "developing countries," or the Two-Thirds World, from Communism was to offer them something positive. Independence, he wrote, was coming.

Colonialism is on the way out as a relationship among peoples. The sole question is one of time and method. I think we should handle it so as to win adherents to Western values. . . . To make use of the spirit of nationalism we must show for it a genuine sympathy.

As for Churchill's own role in this, Eisenhower suggested that not only could the prime minister set out the benefits that could thereby accrue, but

[i]f you then say that twenty-five years from now, every last one of the colonies (excepting military bases) should have been offered a right to self-government and determination [underlined in original], you would electrify the world.

The sheer positivity of Eisenhower's idea shines through: "The kind of talk that I am thinking of would seek to put the whole matter in such a light as to gain us friends—to be positive rather than negative."

This was something that Britain and the United States could achieve together. Playing on Churchill's memories of the 1940s, he added that the two countries "found that fellowship in war, and we must equally try to find it in peace."

Not until August 8 did Churchill reply—after many of the events discussed in the rest of this chapter.

After dealing with these issues, Churchill replied to Eisenhower's great idea. It is incredibly relevant to the debate about Churchill now happening in the 2020s, and shows the massive conceptual gulf between the two men—Eisenhower the protagonist of colonial freedom and the free world, and Churchill, for all his astonishing understanding of twentieth-century technology and the global threat posed by nuclear bombs, someone who in other respects was still in the Victorian era of his youth.

> *I read with great interest all that you have written to me about what is called colonialism, namely: bringing forward backward races and opening up the jungles. I was brought up to be proud of much that we had done. Certainly in India, with all its history, religion and ancient forms of despotic rule, Britain has a story to tell which will look quite well against the background of the coming hundred years.*

Needless to say, that is very much *not* what Indians have felt since their independence in 1947.

Churchill had to confess that British policy was moving toward independence—Ceylon (now Sri Lanka) gained its freedom in 1954. But these were not his personal views:

> *In this I must admit that I am a laggard. I am a bit sceptical [sic] about universal suffrage for the Hottentots even if refined by proportional representation. The British and American Democracies were slowly and painfully forged and even they are not perfect yet. I shall certainly have to choose another topic for my swan song: I think I will stick to the old one "The Unity of the English-speaking peoples." With that all will work out well.*

The obvious and main reaction to this should, of course, be astonishment that Churchill's view of empire was unchanged from his now very distant youth. Reading such opinions in the 2020s is shocking.

But overlooked is his extraordinary opinion of the "English-speaking peoples" in itself, in his usage unfortunate since he is referring to white people only. He perceived Anglo-American unity in wholly archaic terms. Furthermore—and politically this is the crucial factor—*he saw it in terms that the Americans rejected.*

The point about Eisenhower is not that he was simply anti-Communist but that he was *pro-democracy* and pro-freedom. The West, to him, had, as he had written to Churchill, standards and values. Because he believed in those things, he wanted the newly liberated peoples of the world to enjoy them as well. Not only that, but a free and prosperous people would naturally wish to align with the West because they too had come to share those ideas for themselves.

In January 1957 Britain would have a prime minister—Harold Macmillan—who grasped all this completely. By his retirement in 1963, most of the British Empire had been given its independence—nine years after Eisenhower's letter, not twenty-five. (And enormous tribute must also be paid to Queen Elizabeth II, who played a pivotal role in turning empire into Commonwealth.) Come 1989 it was the soft-power ideal of freedom rather than World War III that ended the Cold War, and without the nuclear Armageddon that Churchill rightly feared. In all this Eisenhower and Macmillan understood the modern world, and, sadly for his posthumous reputation today, Churchill did not.

And what kind of "special relationship" was it if the two sides understood it so differently? America wanted Britain to give independence to its colonies and to join with the new Europe being formed just across the English Channel. On both these issues, Churchill said no, which makes ludicrous the notion of him as an American poodle by revisionist historians. Yes, he believed deeply in the English-speaking peoples, but how the English-speaking United States saw the world was utterly different, as Eisenhower made so very clear.

We must now return chronologically to the main narrative and to the events of July 1954, in which we see a different Churchill, the far-seeing statesman who understood what nuclear weapons could destroy.

Did Churchill actually contemplate resignation? The American ambassador, Winthrop Aldrich, put an extraordinary hypothesis to the president, namely that the prime minister had "actually threatened to form a coalition government with the opposition for the purpose of insuring peace if his present colleagues should be unwilling to support him," something Aldrich thought might happen given the country's "existing fears" of what would happen in the event of "atomic warfare." This was, in fact, never in the cards, but it does demonstrate how febrile the emotion had become. Eden, whose health had never recovered from the botched operation the previous year, now literally went to bed!

On July 25 Molotov himself inadvertently solved the problem of the Molotov telegram. The Soviets called for a pan-European conference, with the United States also to attend, to settle matters of collective security. This was, historians agree, an attempt to scupper the prospect, unwelcome to Moscow, of a rearmed Germany within the planned European Defense Community.

So on July 26 Churchill informed his Cabinet colleagues that the Soviet offer created a "new situation." This meant that consequently he was "satisfied that he could not proceed with his proposal for a bilateral meeting with the Russians while this suggestion of a much larger meeting of Foreign Ministers was being publicly canvassed."

The Cabinet crisis was over—all thought of Churchill now engaging in bilateral diplomacy was now "in abeyance."

As Kevin Ruane rightly comments, "For three weeks, Churchill's brazen and bull-headed behaviour had brought the government close to extinction. Now he pulled back from the brink as did his opponents in collective and relieved reaction." There would be no split. And so consequently they nodded through the *real* huge, epoch-making decision after what the Cabinet Secretary noted was a "short discussion" that Britain "should possess a stock of the most up-to-date thermo-nuclear weapons." The next day, on July 28, the formal assent was given and the United Kingdom entered the age of the hydrogen bomb in 1957.

On July 27 Churchill told the House of Commons that his plans to meet the Soviets were now postponed. His official biographer, Sir Martin Gilbert, has concluded that as a result, "Churchill's last great foreign policy initiative was at an end."

In that he never got his bilateral meeting, that is true, but recent historians are also correct in saying that he continued his policy of détente. And here, as we shall see in the next chapter, he was successful.

13

Vietnam and the First Step to a Third World War

How many people know that Eisenhower might, if things had turned out differently, have taken the United States into the war in Vietnam? Today he is praised for keeping the United States *out* of Vietnam, and this is one of the many reasons why his presidency is now regarded by historians—as well as those with fond memories of the 1950s—as one of the best.

But in fact he wanted to take his country *into* a possible war, albeit not at all like the conflict that we remember, which led to thousands of dead young Americans, civil unrest, and in 1975 complete failure—so many lives wasted.

It is even more likely that people do not know that this is in largest measure because of *Winston Churchill.* Most are not even aware that it was a possibility, that Britain would enter a coalition under US leadership, designed either to prevent the war from spreading, or if need be, to join battle with the forces of the Viet Minh. It could have been like the Korean War all over again, but this time, so Eisenhower and others hoped, with a much more satisfactory outcome: Communism at least halted if not defeated altogether.

The significant backdrop to the discussions on Vietnam—or Indochina as it was often described, including Laos and Cambodia—between the United Kingdom and United States was the disintegration of the French position in Vietnam, and in particular the epic battle between Viet Minh forces with the besieged occupiers of Dien Bien Phu in March–May. (Look at a map: Dien Bien Phu is in the north.) Alongside that was the international conference in Geneva on Indochina April–July, to which the Chinese had been invited even though they were not recognized as the legitimate government of China by the United States—an act that had to wait until Nixon's famous visit to Beijing some years into the future.

And importantly, although Britain had no direct stake in the Vietnam conflict, the United Kingdom was represented at the talks in Switzerland, and by far one of the key players was Anthony Eden, as foreign secretary, who was arguably unlucky not to have been given a Nobel

Prize for Peace, as the success of the conference was very much of his making. However, when the conference began, its happy ending was not predicted, and the atmosphere would be tense right through until the conclusion.

The Americans were paying for much of the forlorn French effort to keep Vietnam together—still a very slender possibility, until Dien Bien Phu fell. (When it did, the Geneva decision to split the country in two still left southern Vietnam to defend against the Communists in the north.) No less than 80 percent of the cost of the war was paid by the United States, not by the French.

This was colossally expensive, and from the point of view of many in Congress, a burden of support that the United States was paying alone. This was not popular, and the Eisenhower administration naturally wanted to gain recruits to help the American effort in Vietnam.

(America had subsidized most of the Korean War, but there had at least been soldiers from other countries, the United Kingdom fully included. It was a United Nations–mandated conflict, begun when the Soviets were boycotting the Security Council—now in 1954 that was very much no longer the case. There would be no United Nations mandate for action in Indochina.)

And to the United States, it was not just Vietnam at stake. We now know of the *domino theory*, which argued that if Vietnam fell, so too could the neighboring countries of Laos and Cambodia—and maybe even farther afield. As Dulles confided to Admiral James Radford, the chairman of the Joint Chiefs of Staff (a war hero and former commander of the US fleet in the Pacific), "We could lose Europe, Asia and Africa all at once if we don't watch out."

This was of course hyperbole. But as the French position at Dien Bien Phu became ever more perilous, Eisenhower and his administration decided that the best way forward was a coalition—presumably similar to the one that had contained Communism in Korea—to help the French, the fear being that if the French lost at Dien Bien Phu they might lose heart and evacuate all of Vietnam to the victorious Viet Minh.

There was much debate within the administration in Washington on where next to proceed. Congress had to be won over as well.

Ironically, as American historians such as William Hitchcock have discovered, the United States was much more worried than the French—including the chairman of the Joint Chiefs, Admiral Radford. So on March 26, 1954, Radford, an American commander, asked the French to ask Eisenhower for the United States to send military intervention, in particular massive air strikes to help at Dien Bien Phu.

Clearly unknown to Radford, Eisenhower had been doing some thinking of his own. Not for nothing was he an experienced and successful former military commander—he was well aware, for example, that air power alone would be unlikely to repel the Viet Minh and lift the siege.

His first thinking had been done back in January, in particular with his key wartime colleague Walter Bedell Smith, who had been his Chief of Staff from 1942 to 1945, US ambassador to the USSR 1946 to 1948, and director of the CIA 1950 to 1953, and was now Eisenhower's point man at the State Department as undersecretary of state—in other words, while in a technically junior position, in fact a major player and a man with the utter confidence of his president.

Eisenhower had asked him to contemplate what he described as an "area plan" for Southeast Asia. This, the president suggested, entailed "including alternative lines of action to be taken in case of a reverse in Indochina." Interestingly, historians may well be correct in thinking that Bedell Smith did not fully buy into the domino hypothesis. Their evidence is what Bedell Smith—as mentioned, a former CIA director—told a private meeting of senators from the Foreign Relations Committee a month later.

"Even at the worst," he suggested to them, "part of Indochina can be lost without losing the rest of South-East Asia." This of course disagreed with the domino theory as clearly held by Radford and Dulles. Bedell Smith continued, "One can think of the possibility of an area defense pact which might include Thailand as the bastion, Burma and possibly Cambodia and part of Indochina—and maybe some part of it could be lost without disastrous effect."

Eisenhower biographer William Hitchcock has suggested that in so telling the senators, Bedell Smith would have known the mind of the president when he did so. And developments suggest that this interpretation might be correct.

Along with the military situation and the dire French predicament, Eisenhower realized that there was a wider picture as well, as he wrote to Dulles on March 24, "We should not get involved in fighting in Indochina unless there were the political preconditions necessary for a successful outcome."

Eisenhower was fully cognizant of the difficulties involved, and this guided his thinking as he discussed the options with his team. Ideally, he said at the National Security Council meeting on March 25, any American involvement in the war would need United Nations approval and an invitation from the lawful government of Vietnam—not to mention congressional agreement as well, which, as he told his colleagues, it would be "simply academic to imagine otherwise."

This, the president realized, was all extremely unlikely. So he came to an idea that drew on not just his experience as Supreme Allied Commander during the Second World War, but also his immediate prior post as the military head of NATO. This would be, in effect, war by coalition, which was exactly what Bedell Smith had hinted to the senators the previous month.

Indeed, Eisenhower now suggested that America put together a coalition of "governments and nations who might be approached to assist." Those he had in mind were the United Kingdom, France, Australia, New Zealand, the Philippines, and other free Southeast Asian nations. This would in effect be a regional collective security establishment that could then give support to the beleaguered French.

However, what did Secretary of State Dulles—the man so disliked by Churchill—make of all this?

Dulles outlined his thinking on March 29 to the Overseas Press Club in New York:

> *Under the conditions of today, the imposition of South-East Asia of the political system of Communist Russia and its Chinese Communist ally, by whatever means, would be a grave threat to the whole free community. The United States feels that that possibility should not be passively accepted, but should be met by united action. This might*

involve serious risks. But these risks are far less than those that will face us a few years from now, if we dare not be resolute today.

Much debate has taken place since then on exactly what Dulles implied by the words "united action." And did he agree with his president? Not long after, in a television interview, Eisenhower struck what could be argued as a subtly different tone:

I can conceive of no greater danger to America than to be employing its own ground forces, and any other kind of forces, in great numbers around the world, meeting each little situation as it arises. . . . What we are trying to do is to make our friends strong enough to take care of local situations by themselves, with the financial, the moral, the political and, certainly, only where our own vital interests demand any military help.

This is a more nuanced approach than that of Dulles. But precisely what both the president and the secretary of state meant in their respective utterances was absolutely crucial to their listeners—no more so than to those across the Atlantic, in France, about to face what could be humiliation; and the United Kingdom, worried about what one could describe as a very different and far deadlier domino approach, as we will see shortly.

In the end it was only Australia that would send forces to Vietnam, and that several years later; in 1954 there was not even the army of American soldiers who would eventually come and fight, only what were known as advisers. But they were there, as anyone who has read Graham Greene's great novel *The Quiet American* will know. Vietnam was not yet the bloodbath that it would become.

It has been said that the reason why President Lyndon Johnson did not attend Churchill's funeral in 1965 is that he was angry at Prime Minister Harold Wilson's absolute refusal to send British troops to Vietnam, or indeed to become involved in the war in any way. Eisenhower *was* at the event, but, while now a former US president, attended as a private individual, a friend since 1941. Vice President Hubert Humphrey represented the United States instead. So Wilson's brave stand—refusing to do in Vietnam what the British had done over Korea—was a distinct glitch in what was still called the "special relationship," a refusal by the United Kingdom to fulfill a request from its American ally. (And as we know, the sky did not fall in as a result . . .)

But much less known, if at all, is that *Churchill refused to let Britain join the Vietnam War as well*, all the way back in 1954. And this, one could argue, as for example does Kevin Ruane, who has written in detail on the Geneva Conference, is connected to the very understandable British horror of the United Kingdom being destroyed in a nuclear strike from the USSR. Vietnam and the prospect of annihilation were closely linked in Churchill's mind, and that of his military advisers the Chiefs of Staff. As they and Cabinet ministers now realized, while the Soviets did not yet have the ability to launch hydrogen bombs against the United States—for at least another five years into the future—the United Kingdom could be hit straightaway.

As Anthony Eden told a rather alarmed Cabinet meeting on March 22, Eisenhower's New Look policy, of such weapons being part of legitimate policy, the "US will soon assume that *any* action by them is atomic. They will have all their armaments attuned & fitted for atomic weapons *only*." Dulles's speech a week later only confirmed their fears.

In particular, one can argue that the British now saw a different kind of domino theory emerging. The war in Vietnam might trigger Chinese intervention, and were *that* to be the case, the United States might launch a nuclear attack on China. And of course once such weapons had been employed, World War III might be just around the corner, with US missile bases in the eastern part of England a natural target for Soviet counterattack on the West.

Dulles and Eisenhower now had another kind of domino effect in mind. Worrying as they did about how to persuade Congress to authorize even more money for the fight against Communism in Southeast Asia, they decided that Britain might be the key, as they put it, to getting a coalition together that would persuade those holding the congressional purse strings that the United States was not going to be in Vietnam alone.

Unfortunately for the American administration, the notion that Britain would automatically come to the aid of the United States—as it had done in 1950 in Korea—was already illusory. Both Eden and the Chiefs of Staff advised the Cabinet that such action would be folly:

Any direct action ... by the armed forces of any external nation ... would probably result in Chinese intervention, with the danger that this might ultimately lead to global war. . . . Our influence should therefore be used against these more dangerous forms of deeper United States involvement. Britain would therefore not join the United States in Vietnam.

And here Kevin Ruane's interpretation surely also blasts a hole in the revisionist interpretation that Churchill was America's poodle and that the United Kingdom had been reduced to being a mere satrap in the great American empire, compelled to obey whenever the United States demanded.

Consequently, Anglo-American relations reached one of their lowest points since the Second World War—and on the watch of Winston Churchill, the great guardian, the inventor even, of the "special relationship."

"Normally," Ruane continues, "Churchill would have been first in line behind the Americans." Not this time, however! And it was because the prime minister realized the dangers into which such action would place his country—nuclear destruction. But as we shall see, the effect of all this was not to persuade Churchill to join the siren-song chorus demanding total nuclear disarmament, *but for Britain to have its own hydrogen bomb*, a British deterrent independent of that of the United States.

And how this proves a thesis that Britain had lost its independence and existed only to obey its superiors in Washington now surely boggles the mind. These are not the reactions of a slave. Furthermore, the thesis that Churchill subsumed the United Kingdom to American dictates whereas brave and foresight-filled Eden stood alone for British interests is also untenable. For while in Bermuda Eden had been worried that Churchill would concede too much to Eisenhower, on the issue of involvement in Vietnam, both prime minister and foreign secretary stood shoulder to shoulder, together in full accord.

So we can say that there was a difference of understanding of what any kind of military action in Indochina would involve. A 1950s specialist, William Hitchcock, is surely right to say:

> *Eisenhower, a lifelong student of strategy, knew that deterrence could succeed in keeping the peace only if it were backed by a willingness to use force. He wanted to keep America out of war, but perhaps the best way to do that was to prepare for it.*

Deterrence theory agrees fully with this, and it was precisely this kind of strategic thinking that led the British, later that year, to prepare to have nuclear weapons of their own. But as of 1954 they did *not* possess such force, and that was to weigh considerably on their decision-making.

And Eisenhower needed British support, especially as he and Dulles realized in talking to Congress, whose approval, as we saw, was essential for any US action of any kind to proceed. This became crystal clear on April 3, when Dulles and Radford met with leading members of Congress. It has been immortalized as "the day we didn't go to war," but the reality is subtler. What Dulles reported back to the president was, "Congress would be quite prepared to go along on some vigorous action if we were not doing it alone." In effect, historians have interpreted this as saying that "meant Eisenhower and Dulles needed Britain to sign on to united action, and fast."

After consulting with both Dulles and the counsel to the State Department, Eisenhower then dispatched a major epistle to Churchill on April 4 with the hope that Britain would indeed join in the coalition that he now wished to form.

He was rather over-optimistic on the French at Dien Bien Phu. But should France fail, he was deeply pessimistic on how things would then unfold. He reminded Churchill that the "French alone cannot see this thing through" and if Communism prevailed, "the ultimate effect on our and your global strategic position with the consequent shift in the power ratio throughout Asia and the Pacific could be disastrous, and, I know, unacceptable to you and me." Taking the domino effect to its extreme, he foresaw a scenario in which not only would Thailand, Burma, and

Indonesia fall to Communism, but Malaya, Australia, and New Zealand would be in danger as well. (From the late 1940s to mid-1960s, the British were fighting against Communist guerrilla forces in Malaya—and successfully as it turned out, with therefore a much happier outcome for all concerned than the American experience in Vietnam.) Not only that, but the future of France as a great power was itself at stake.

Eisenhower envisaged a coalition including Britain and the United States, France, Australia, New Zealand, Thailand, and the Philippines. And should China menace Hong Kong, the United States would stand with the United Kingdom.

This, he explained carefully to Churchill, would be "a new ad hoc grouping or coalition of nations which have a vital concern in the checking of Communist expansion in the area." He continued:

The important thing is that the coalition must be strong and it must be willing to join the fight if necessary. I do not envisage the need of any appreciable ground forces on your or our part. If the members of the alliance are sufficiently resolute it should be able to make clear to the Chinese Communists that the continuation of their material support to the Viet Minh will inevitably lead to the growing power of the forces arrayed against them.

"My colleagues and I," he added, "are deeply aware of the risks."

Along with a promise to send a senior American to London, he concluded by appealing to Churchill's bold stand in the 1930s and the failure of France to withstand invasion in 1940:

In many ways the situation corresponds to that which you describe so brilliantly in the second chapter of "Their Finest Hour," when history made clear the 1940 breakthrough [of Germany into France] should have been challenged before the blow fell. . . . If I may refer to history, we failed to halt Hirohito, Mussolini and Hitler by not acting in unity and in time. That marked the beginning of many years of stark tragedy and desperate peril. May it not be that our nations have learned something from the lesson?

Parallels from history are dangerous things. In 1956 Eden would see the Egyptian dictator Nasser as another Mussolini, and thereby involve Britain—with Israel and France—in one of the greatest foreign policy disasters in British history, at Suez. By not aiding the United Kingdom, Eisenhower demonstrated that he saw no parallels with the 1930s. One could argue, though, that Eisenhower was as wrong over Ho Chi Minh as Eden was over Nasser. Neither man planned world conquests on the scale of a Hitler. Both leaders were nationalists, fighting against the relics of colonialism in their countries.

Ho, as a Communist, did share the same ideological loyalties on the universal rightness of his beliefs as those possessed in both the USSR and China, but that did not make *him* into a Hirohito figure. Nasser wanted the entire Middle East to be free from the old yokes of the past—indeed, it has been stated that he and Neguib were the first native Egyptians to rule that nation since the Pharaohs, as the Romans, Byzantines, Islamic Caliphs, and Ottomans were all outsiders as much as the British. But in essence it was their *own* countries that Ho and Nasser wanted to liberate, not to wage a campaign of Nazi or Japanese imperialist foreign conquest.

Similar parallels were made in 2003 about Saddam Hussein being a new Hitler figure, and that to allow him to stay in power was to return to the appeasement of the 1930s. Whether or not such examples are true depends on whether the invasion of Iraq was a good decision or bad, but it does show that one has to be careful when using the past to justify decisions in the present.

In 1954 Churchill spoke of his wish to have good relations with the USSR as "easement"—was that the wicked appeasement of Munich under another name? There were certainly right-wing Conservative Party members of Parliament on the backbenches of the House of Commons who thought so—the same ideological wing of the party of which Churchill had been a member pre-1939. History is replete with ironies.

So in 1954 Britain and the United States disagreed in one direction (over Vietnam), and in 1956 they would diverge in another (over Egypt). The key takeaway here is that while everyone knows that Eden transgressed the "special relationship" over Suez, *so in 1954 did Churchill over Vietnam*. As Churchill confided at this time to his physician Lord Moran,

"I am more worried by the hydrogen bomb than by all my other worries put together."

So while the Americans were thinking about Indochina and the containment of Chinese Communism, the British were scared that if matters got seriously out of control, Soviet nuclear weapons would be wiping out English cities.

And this is why it is right to argue that the timing of Eisenhower's missive to Churchill was unfortunate—the issues of Indochina and nuclear holocaust were getting enmeshed in the British mind.

Not only that, but Eisenhower's rather sanguine view of April 4 was soon proved to be out of date—in fact, that very day. The French were now so perturbed about their position in Dien Bien Phu that they requested American air strikes, and immediately.

But as Eisenhower understood, constitutionally this was impossible—congressional authorization would be needed, and that would most likely not be forthcoming. In essence, the French were trying to push the United States into precipitate action, with all possibilities of dire consequences to follow, including for Eisenhower's coalition plan. For the president and his plan, this was all bad news, because his intended coalition would take time to form, and time is what the French had now refused to grant him. His strategy, as outlined to Churchill, was now beginning to unravel.

The National Security Council on April 6 was thus an understandably gloomy affair. But Eisenhower stood firm on his views, apparently uttering them with "great emphasis" to his colleagues. There "was no possibility whatever of US unilateral intervention in Indochina," he told them, "and we had best face that fact." Even Dulles now agreed that the president's coalition idea had merit, if it could be strong enough so that "military intervention might prove unnecessary."

After much discussion, with hawks such as Vice President Richard Nixon hoping against hope that military action was still on the table, Eisenhower held his ground. He "expressed warm approval for the idea of a political organization which would have for its purpose the defense of Southeast Asia even if Indochina should be lost. In any case, the creation of such an organization for defense would be better than emergency military action." The very existence of such a group would in and of itself work successfully to deter Chinese aggression.

This is not the domino theory. But what did Eisenhower then talk about the very next day at a press briefing?—*the domino theory*. In other words, in just a few minutes the president undid all the good work he had just accomplished at the National Security Council, and scared witless everyone listening to him, not just those in Washington, but, more importantly, those across the Atlantic, Britain very fully included.

As he put it to one of his questioners:

> *First of all, you have the specific value of a locality in its production of materials that the world needs. Then you have the possibility that many human beings pass under a dictatorship that is inimical to the free world. Finally you have broader considerations that might follow what you would call the "falling domino" principle. You have a row of dominoes set up, you knock over the first one, and what will happen to the last one is the certainty that it will go over very quickly.*

And just to compound everything, he even gave an example of what would happen to Asia were Indochina to fall: "[T]he possible consequences of the loss are incalculable to the free world."

So the private Eisenhower, talking moderately at the National Security Council, and the public president, spreading gloom to the world's media, were now in direct contradiction with each other.

Needless to say, which of the two was the *real* Eisenhower—indeed if there was even such a thing as a genuine Eisenhower—was not at all clear to the British. This became evident when the Cabinet met on April 6.

Eden told his colleagues that while the *concept* of a coalition had its merits, the problem was that the real motive behind the idea was that the Americans wanted a security organization with which to intimidate the Chinese before the Geneva Conference on Indochina began. And then he put his finger on the nub of British fears:

> *Moreover, if China were not intimidated by the threat, the coalition would be compelled either to withdraw ignominiously or to embark*

on warlike action against China. This would give the Chinese every excuse for invoking the Sino-Soviet treaty, and might lead to world war.

Might lead to world war—the stakes could not possibly be higher. In the discussion that took place, unnamed Cabinet ministers were recorded as saying:

There was no indication whether the Americans had it in mind that the air action in Indochina, or against China itself, would include the use of atomic or hydrogen bombs. . . . President Eisenhower had suggested that the preparations for the Geneva Conference would afford a convenient pretext for Mr Dulles' visit to London. The British public would, however, connect it with the current American tests of hydrogen bombs, and would expect it to lead to some further pronouncement on that question.

And so the government would therefore also ask this question of Dulles when he came.

Churchill could see his own dilemma—his passionate belief in the "special relationship" and his deep concern about the effects of hydrogen bombs. He felt that the government should stall, which is what the Cabinet agreed.

The prime minister then wrote a carefully non-committal letter to Eisenhower. The Cabinet, he told the president, had been "giving it a great deal of thought. It is however a topic which raises many problems for us and I am sure you will not expect us to give a hurried decision."

The Cabinet's doubts were made plain to Dulles when he came to London at Churchill's request for talks on April 11. It was not merely the Eisenhower of the press conference that so disturbed them, but also the results of the latest hydrogen bomb test in the Pacific that we saw earlier.

So while Dulles was talking about a US/UK-led coalition of eight further nations to guarantee security in Indochina and act as a deterrent to possible Chinese aggression, what the Cabinet was actually hearing was the danger of a nuclear strike on English soil.

Eden, leading for the British side, ostensibly prevaricated, but it was clear that the United Kingdom would in reality not be interested in joining Eisenhower's plan. What Eden suggested as the alternative was in fact what eventually happened—a Communist-led North Vietnam and a free South Vietnam. And this, Eden argued, was a realistic solution and would be achievable at the international conference soon to meet at Geneva, a gathering that would end up choosing Eden's peaceful option.

Speaking for the government, Eden was alarmed that "injudicious military decisions" by the United States could undo all possible avenues to peace. As for threatening Communist China with nuclear attack, Eden averred that threats could never be "sufficiently potent to make China swallow so humiliating a rebuff as the abandonment of the Vietminh without any face-saving concession in return."

In other words, the British fear, one that as we have seen also dominated Churchill's constant thoughts, was that the American plan, far from bringing peace and security, could in fact lead to nuclear war.

Just before going on to Geneva, Eden met Dulles at a NATO meeting in Paris on April 23 (there had been some worries about possible Soviet troop actions in Austria—still under four-power occupation—but these had proved to be false alarms). The French had used the opportunity of the likely imminent fall of Dien Bien Phu to pressure the Americans into sending military support. Both Dulles and Admiral Radford, chairman of the Joint Chiefs, realized that the siege situation was hopeless. Dulles used this as an excuse now to ask Eden in effect for Britain to stop dithering and join the coalition.

He was able to do so because both he and Eden were at the NATO gathering. Dulles flat out asked the foreign secretary if Britain would stand with America in supporting the French. If so, Eisenhower would ask Congress for "war powers" for a massive US armed intervention in Vietnam to aid the flagging French. Eden prevaricated and immediately called a special Cabinet/Chiefs of Staff meeting back in London the next morning.

Naturally, Eden felt that the US proposal had to be turned down, given the immense risk of it spreading to an altogether wider war. He then outlined his partition plan, splitting the country into two zones divided along the 17th Parallel—a divide that became famous when the Vietnam War later broke out in earnest. It was inevitable, he told his colleagues, that "large parts of Indo-China should fall under Communist control," and partition would recognize that. Eden's idea was to be the one finally adopted at the Geneva talks, and although it was not meant to be the final border, it was in effect creating the communist North Vietnam and the capitalist South Vietnam, which were to fight the subsequent conflict until the Communists prevailed in 1975 and reunited the country under their rule.

What is interesting is that Churchill agreed with Eden. As he told his colleagues, Britain would "clearly be ill-advised to encourage the Americans to take precipitate military action." With this everyone at the meeting agreed.

The cabinet then had to be reconvened to discuss the news that the Americans would launch air strikes to defend the beleaguered Dien Bien Phu garrison if the British agreed.

This was the very stuff of British nightmares. Eden spoke for all his colleagues when he outlined a scenario in which the Chinese would then intervene to help the Viet Minh, followed by the United States launching a nuclear strike against the Chinese, the result of which would be "a grave risk that the Soviet Union would feel obliged to intervene." That would, Eden declared, be "the first step towards a third world war."

And once more *Churchill backed this diagnosis*. As he put it, the request for Britain to back US military intervention in Vietnam "was in effect to aid in misleading Congress approving a military operation [at Dien Bien Phu] which would itself be ineffective and might well bring the world to the verge of a major war." Speaking just for himself, the prime minister "had no doubts that this request must be rejected."

Eden was given the difficult task of breaking this news to Dulles— with *carte blanche* from Churchill on "how to play the hand." Churchill was fully aware of the effect that all this was having on Anglo-American relations when he telegrammed Eden to say, "I sympathise with you in all your trials which are also ours. I have a feeling things have turned more sour. Sour is an understatement." Once again, the idea in revisionist circles that Churchill was some kind of American poodle is proved to be a serious misinterpretation of the past; if a canine analogy is suitable, Churchill was being his bulldog self and putting the security of the United Kingdom ahead of the wishes of the United States.

This is not how Eisenhower saw it. As he wrote to one of his closest personal friends, he despised Britain's "morbid obsession that any positive move on the part of the free world may bring upon us World War III," thereby unknowingly echoing the very fears expressed at the British Cabinet. But the United States, Eisenhower maintained, would not act unilaterally—he still hankered after his coalition idea, and this would prove to be vital.

The rather forlorn French request for aid had rattled some in Washington, including a key member of the National Security Council. And astonishingly, this discussion brought forth from the president sentiments similar to Churchill's. Eisenhower realized something very important, telling his colleagues that if the United States did send in forces to aid France, "we would in the eyes of many Asiatic peoples merely replace French colonialism with American colonialism." In this Eisenhower was not only correct but unknowingly prophetic, because it is of course exactly what happened when the United States did intervene in the 1960s: the charge of both colonialism and imperialism that was laid against the United States in the war in Indochina.

He saw this himself, telling his colleagues on the National Security Council: "We would soon lose all our significant support in the free world. We would be everywhere accused of imperialistic ambitions." If the United States were so stupid as to act on its own, it "would mean a general war with China and perhaps with the USSR."

This idea of World War III, which he had dismissed as needless British cowardice, now actually came from Eisenhower's own lips! But the key difference is that to Eisenhower this contingency referred only to *unilateral* American action—the coalition of which he still dreamed would be a very different affair.

He still hoped to persuade Churchill and therefore dispatched Admiral Radford to see the prime minister at Chequers on April 26. Eden was worried that Churchill might fall sway to American entreaties. But he mistook his man—this time the prime minister would stand firm.

Radford certainly did his utmost to fulfill Eisenhower's request to get Churchill back on their side. Should Britain and the United States not come together, he told the prime minister, such "failure . . . would be a great victory for the Communists and a turning point in history. . . . NATO itself might well be destroyed . . . Australia and New Zealand would be threatened. Japanese thoughts would turn to Asiatic Communism with which they would believe the future to lie. . . . This was the critical moment at which to make a stand against China," and every delay would only make Communism stronger.

In addition to outlining other horrors, he offered a diplomatic bribe—if Britain collaborated, then the United States would no longer be neutral in relation to the United Kingdom's interests in Egypt.

But Churchill now showed that while he was as passionately pro-American as ever—indeed in the "special relationship"—other factors had intervened. What he told Radford is fascinating, as it shows beyond peradventure that the nuclear issue superseded everything else in his thinking. While the current circumstances might indeed be "a critical moment in history,"

[t]he British people would not be easily influenced by what happened in the distant jungles of SE Asia; but they did know there was a powerful American base in East Anglia [Eastern England] and that war with China, who would invoke the Sino-Russian Pact, might mean an assault by Hydrogen bombs on these islands. We could not commit ourselves at this moment, when all these matters were about to be discussed at Geneva, to a policy which might lead by slow stages to catastrophe.

Now, he reminded Radford, it might even be possible for the Russians to drop hydrogen bombs over the United States, albeit "given the present state of Russian aviation, the immediate Russian target was more likely to be East Anglia or London than the United States." Once more Churchill made his plea for a Great Power meeting, what he called "conversations at the centre," which would, he hoped, "not lead either to appeasement . . . or to an ultimatum, but they would be calculated to bring home to the

Russians the full implications of Western strength and to impress upon them the folly of war."

Churchill, very nicely for historians, then spelled out how he combined his devotion to the Anglo-American relationship and his refusal to be involved in Vietnam:

> *The prime minister thought nothing more important than the close alliance of the English-speaking peoples and the continued effective cooperation of Great Britain and the United States. He had devoted a great part of his life and strength to this end. But we could not allow ourselves to be committed against our judgement to a policy which might lead to our destruction, the more so when we believed that the action which the Americans now proposed was almost certain to be ineffective. Geneva, in short, would sort everything out.*

Radford, who was flying back the next day to see Eisenhower, would thus be bringing the president bad news. As he left Chequers, he had one last salvo: The risks were exaggerated and delay "could only bring further misfortunes." For Eisenhower, "[c]ooperation with Great Britain was the keystone of his policy and he was certain that without it both the United States and the United Kingdom would drift to disaster."

Churchill had stuck to his guns—to the profound relief of Eden, currently in Geneva aiming not for nuclear conflagration but for a peaceful agreement on Indochina. And now it was vital that the British had a hydrogen bomb of their own, so that never again could American action threaten death and destruction on English soil.

In the United States, it was clear to Eisenhower that the British would not participate. Needless to add, he was disappointed. But despite this, he remained loyal to his convictions—either a coalition or no war.

When his National Security Council met on April 29, the hawks around the table were not pleased. Harold Stassen, who directed American foreign aid, was furious, wanting unilateral action whatever France or Britain thought.

Eisenhower showed himself the world statesman for which he is now lauded. If, he informed his colleagues on the National Security Council,

America intervened on its own, that "would mean a general war with China and perhaps with the USSR"—the very World War III for which he had just condemned Britain's morbid fear. Furthermore—and this is fascinating to read in the light of later events under Kennedy and Johnson in Vietnam—such precipitate unilateral intervention "amounted to an attempt to police the entire world." As *The Age of Eisenhower* author William Hitchcock quotes him as saying, "We should soon lose all our significant support in the free world. We should be everywhere accused of imperialistic ambitions" (exactly the crime of which America was indicted in the 1960s).

Stassen was furious. Doing nothing, to him, "would be tantamount to giving Britain a veto on US action in Southeast Asia."

In one sense this was correct—Churchill and Eden, by refusing to let Britain be involved in a coalition war in Vietnam, had *in that sense* vetoed American action. But in reality that is because Eisenhower had made their approval a condition for war, by rejecting the unilateralism of the hard-liners in the United States who were longing for an anti-Communist crusade.

While Churchill was not privy to such discussions, he was right to realize that the world was now in a dangerous place if it did not actively pursue a policy of peace. On May 4 he expounded to the newly formed Defense Policy Committee, which consisted not only of key Cabinet ministers but also of the Chiefs of Staff of the armed forces. His views also show that he still had a fundamentally optimistic interpretation of the USSR, and a pessimistic outlook on the United States, as we see here:

> *The prime minister said that there was very little doubt that the Soviet government would seek to avoid war for so long as they continued to be able to achieve so many of their aims without it. . . . So long as this situation continued, there seemed to be very little risk of world war—unless the United States should succumb to the temptation to bring matters to a head before the Russians had built up their strength in atomic weapons and their power to deliver them against targets in North America.*

This is what he had discussed with Radford: At the moment the Soviets could only strike the United Kingdom, but their technology would soon reach the United States, so the possibility of an American preemptive first strike against the USSR was very much on Churchill's mind, and others in the small circle who possessed knowledge of this fact.

As he put it:

> *It was arguable that the United States would better serve their own interests by an early trial of strength with Russia than by committing their forces successively, in different theatres, in support of efforts to check Communist encroachment into the free world. The great question was whether the United States would withstand the temptation to initiate what we would prefer to call a "forestalling" war, rather than a "preventive" war.*

Should such a conflict break out, Britain could not of course remain neutral, and even if the British did try to stay out, "her fate would be determined by it. If Soviet forces overran Europe, the United Kingdom would not go unscathed." This was not morbidity, as Eisenhower had earlier described the British view, but a realistic understanding of the perils that Britain would face should nuclear war erupt.

This was the McCarthy era—as Churchill and his close colleagues on the Defense Policy Committee were all too aware. Today the idea of the United States launching a preemptive nuclear strike on the Soviet Union back then seems far-fetched, if not fantastical. Later in the Cold War the notion of *mutually assured destruction* meant that a nuclear strike was the last thing any American or Soviet leader would want, since no one would survive. Once again, it is surely right to argue that deterrence worked—the World War Three of the doom-mongers never happened precisely because the leaders of both sides were what political scientists call "rational actors" who knew full well that such a conflict would be an Armageddon in which the world would destroy itself.

But when Churchill and the other members of the Defense Policy Committee surveyed news from the United States—the McCarthy witch hunt being especially on their minds—there was, the prime minister felt, "a climate of opinion" in America "which would be favourable to an early trial of strength" with the Soviets. So such a pessimistic view, however extreme, was not altogether without its rationale.

And this is why Britain needed its own nuclear weapons. Only with a *British* hydrogen bomb could the United Kingdom deter the Soviets from launching devastation on East Anglia, and only with possession of such a weapon could the country have any influence over what decisions were made in Washington, DC. The United Kingdom, in other words, would be a player, giving the country, as Churchill put it, "the maintenance of our influence in world councils." Britain would then have the international status to be able to insist on having a voice "in determining the major issue of peace and war."

14

An Obstinate Pig Is the Best I Can Do

CHURCHILL MIGHT HAVE LOST OUT IN HIS DESIRE TO MEET WITH Malenkov and Molotov in Moscow, but he never gave up hoping and his utter conviction that it was the right thing to do. He knew writing to Eisenhower was like banging his head against the proverbial brick wall. But he persisted nonetheless—ending his letter with a commendable sense of self-awareness and impish humor: "I told [Eisenhower's emissary Bedell Smith] to tell you that I was 'an obstinate pig.' Alas, it is the best I can do." (Churchill often drew himself as a pig in his letters to Clementine as a term of endearment. Clearly the pig had other characteristics as well!)

His obstinacy is arguably the reason why he still insisted to his increasingly frantic colleagues that he would not retire, as both they in London and Eisenhower in Washington were keen for him to do. He was not clinging to power for the sake of it—he genuinely believed that he could bring world peace. This was by now forlorn, and Churchill's belief was possibly egotistical, but that does not mean that he was being anything other than sincere.

Despite the setback, his views, he told Eisenhower, were unaltered by the fact that it would now be Foreign Offices [i.e., State Departments], not individuals, that would do the negotiating in the future.

> One has to do one's duty as one sees it from day to day and, as you know, the mortal peril which overhangs the human race is never absent from my thoughts. I am not looking about for the means of making a dramatic exit or finding a suitable Curtain. . . . It will seem astonishing to future generations—such as they may be—that with all that is at stake no attempt was made by personal parley between the Heads of Government to create a union of consenting minds on broad and simple issues.

How about Nixon's trip to see Mao in China? Reagan and Gorbachev holding talks in Reykjavík? Today we take such famous events for granted, and the fact that both turned out to be world changing and historic. What Churchill wanted is *summit diplomacy*, and in this he was ahead of his time. He chided Eisenhower that the president had never met Malenkov, "when all the time [in] the two countries," the United States and USSR, "appalling preparations are being made for measureless mutual destruction." All he had been trying to do was "do my best to take any small practical step in my power to bring about a sensible and serious contact."

The French Parliament rejected the European Defense Community on August 30, 1954, and, contrary to previous fears, the roof did not fall in. In 1955 Germany became part of NATO—which it has been ever since—and a fully sovereign country once more. British and American forces stayed on as NATO troops, and the fear of those in the United Kingdom and other parts of Europe that the United States would withdraw its troops was happily misplaced. Churchill had, in fact, been very favorable to the NATO option when he met with the French prime minister earlier that month—before the vote—so for the United Kingdom the result was more than acceptable.

The transition to the NATO option took up much time and transatlantic correspondence. And in the memoirs and diaries of British politicians of the time, so too did the endless plotting to persuade Churchill finally to retire—with his eightieth birthday looming in November, ministers' thoughts were concentrated heavily on how to give him the opportunity to do so gracefully. Needless to say, he ignored all of it and decided to stay, reconstructing his government in October and placing Harold Macmillan in the key position of Minister of Defense.

His speech to the Conservative Party that year was on the theme of "Peace through Strength." And toward the end of it, he made another peroration in favor of the United States:

I have always thought that the growth of ever closer ties with the United States, to whom we and our sister Commonwealth are bound, by language, by literature, and by law, is one, is the supreme factor in our future and that together we of the English-speaking world may make the world safe for ourselves and everybody else. There is no other case of a nation arriving at the summit of world power, seeking no

territorial gain, but earnestly resolved to use her strength and wealth
in the cause of progress and freedom.

Yet, as we have seen, he was also privately proud of being an "obstinate pig." When it came to something in which he believed deeply, such
as the likelihood of mutually assured destruction and nuclear weapons, or
his wish to have a final parley with Malenkov in Moscow, he was firmly of
independent mind, and not remotely the lickspittle poodle that revisionist historians have often portrayed him. His correspondence with Eisenhower makes this clear. If he was a lapdog, it was a canine with teeth.

But here we come into British culture war territory. As he mentioned
in his Lord Mayor's Banquet speech on November 9:

> *One thing is certain: with the word divided as it is at present, the*
> *freedom of our vast international association of the free peoples can*
> *only be founded upon strength and strength can only be maintained*
> *by unity. The whole foundation of our existence stands on our alliance,*
> *friendship, and an increasing sense of brotherhood with the United*
> *States, and we are also developing increasingly intimate ties with*
> *France, Germany, Italy, and the Low Countries which are stronger*
> *and more practical than any that have yet been devised. From these*
> *solemn and important agreements we hope that we shall be able to*
> *create the peace and strength which will allow time to play its part*
> *and bring together an altogether easier relationship all over the world.*

The "special relationship" is clearly present at the center of his
thoughts. But what were the "increasingly intimate ties" with the nations
in Europe of which he also spoke? What happened? The answer is that
for the rest of his premiership and the whole of Eden's, absolutely nothing
at all happened, while the leaders of Europe were getting together to form
what we now call the European Community.

Only when Harold Macmillan came to power did a British government decide that genuinely "increasingly intimate ties" with Europe were
vital for the United Kingdom. By that time though, Charles de Gaulle
was in power in France, a leader whose hostility to the United States and

suspicion of the United Kingdom as the lackey of the United States was to keep Britain out of the new Europe until 1973, after his retirement and death.

For British people in the 2020s, this is an acute area of disagreement—indeed the equivalent in vehemence and polarization of the culture wars in the United States. Churchill, as mentioned elsewhere in this book, has become a political football—at time of writing his name appears regularly in newspaper articles and letters, claimed with equal passion by both sides of the political debate on the nature of Britain's ties with Europe!

His grandson Sir Nicholas Soames and his great-grandson Hugo Dixon have been stalwarts of the pro-European cause, so in terms of members of Churchill's descendants who have put their heads above the political parapet, their allegiance is abundantly clear. And as is obvious, the Europhile sympathies of your author are entirely with them.

However, in terms of the debate about Churchill among writers and historians, the strange thing is that there is unanimity between the revisionists, who seek to portray Churchill as betraying his country's true interests in favor of being the pawn of the over-mighty United States, and his standard biographers, for whom his vision of the English-speaking peoples is one of his most legitimate claims to greatness, since his obvious affinity for the Anglosphere is a statement of self-evident truth.

This is because the revisionists and defenders, in terms of twenty-first-century culture war politics, are *Eurosceptics*. This is true of two of the most distinguished historians to make their names in writing about Churchill, whom we discussed when looking at the key strategic decisions of World War Two: John Charmley and Andrew Roberts.

In looking at the events of 1940–1941, it is surely the case, as we saw, that Andrew Roberts is entirely right: Britain could not possibly have done a deal with Hitler, America was the only possible means of salvation for Britain, and any loss of power in relation to the United States was a price worth paying, since for the United Kingdom to have been a satrap of the Third Reich would have been infinitely worse. As Churchill realized at Tehran, the United Kingdom had lost out as a Great Power to the United States and the USSR, but in 1945 Britain was free and on the winning side.

But interestingly, when it comes to the 1950s and Churchill's choices, both writers implicitly or otherwise agree that he was right for Britain *not* to have the closer ties with Europe that were now forming, and which more far-sighted Conservatives such as Harold Macmillan were beginning to understand as by far the best way forward for a modern post-war United Kingdom. Give Africa its independence, end the old colonialist mentality, and join in the exciting new developments in Europe—*that* was the future.

The irony is that this was precisely what Eisenhower wanted Britain to do—get closer to Europe and begin the process of decolonization.

What is strange, therefore, is that Churchill was in effect advocating an Anglo-American "special relationship" while being simultaneously engaged in policies completely divergent from what the United States wanted.

How is this poodle-like obeisance portrayed by Churchill's revisionists? This is a statesman going his own way—over Europe, over empire, over nuclear weapons, over bilateral talks with Moscow. On all these key issues, Churchill was in fact very much his own man. And yet no one was louder in proclaiming the centrality of the links between the English-speaking peoples, especially between the United Kingdom and United States, than the same Winston Churchill himself. There is a discrepancy here, between the dream and the reality, which has arguably not had the attention it deserves.

In the United States, Churchill is right to be famous for his magnificent defense of liberty in 1940, and for his understanding of the importance of the United States. It is how he is remembered, and why he remains an icon to this very day. But an icon is perfect, 100 percent correct, and here is where the difficulties begin. There is no nuance with an image.

And that is why a genuine assessment of Churchill is so hard. It is not surprising that it is in the United States where he holds his current godlike status, because in reality for Americans there are only two parts of his life that truly matter: defying Hitler in 1940 and his prophetic description of the post-war world order in his famous Iron Curtain speech on March 5, 1946, the "Sinews of Peace." On both occasions one can legitimately argue that history has shown him emphatically correct, not just, as he once quipped, because he would write the history himself, but because events vindicated him utterly.

But that does not make him perfect. It is not surprising that in the United Kingdom, his home country, his reputation is more nuanced. And the reason should be obvious—in Britain he is also a partisan political figure, someone who changed his political party not once but twice. How you interpret Churchill is inevitably through the prism of your own political views. Plainly that is not the case in the United States, the country where he remains a hero well above the domestic fray.

So in England it is possible to say that he was the greatest Briton who ever lived, and mean that sincerely, yet at the same time admit that he was *not* perfect and over a uniquely long political career of more than six decades, made errors of judgment and, dare one say it, actual mistakes.

Eisenhower was thus on the right side of history when he asked Churchill to make decolonization his swan-song theme in 1954. So too, one hopes, would all of us be today.

And there is a nice irony pointed out by John Charmley that is surely correct. *America had once been a British colony.* The very self-universal suffrage for Hottentots? India freed from oriental despotism by benign British colonial rule? Surely views such as this are not acceptable today, and of course Churchill was very much a man of his time—his future successor, Harold Macmillan, who gave millions of Africans their freedom, was a full twenty years younger than Churchill, and while also born in the nineteenth century, in reality from an altogether different era. Remember that Churchill was originally out of power from *1931* because of his fanatical opposition even for Home Rule for India, and not because of his entirely courageous and visionary opposition to appeasement from Hitler's accession to power two years later in 1933.

This is something that evidently eluded Churchill, with his romantic view of the English-speaking peoples and the fundamental unity that he believed they possessed. In many ways this is historically true—Magna Carta is as revered in the United States as it is in England, and when the revolutionaries in the eighteenth century saw themselves as fighting despotism, it was, as many of them saw it, to establish their inalienable rights as freeborn Englishmen, standing together in defiance of royal tyranny.

There was a view in the 1970s that what Washington and Jefferson and others were trying to achieve is the proper interpretation of the Glorious Revolution of 1689 in Britain, when a group of British politicians and soldiers—including the great John Churchill First Duke of Marlborough—endeavored to get rid of the attempts of King James II to restore absolutism, place his daughter Mary and son-in-law William of Orange on the throne, and thereby consolidate the gains of Parliamentary rule that were supposed to have been finalized after the English Civil War but had fallen in jeopardy. It might be taking this interpretation too far to say that the president of the United States is a correctly understood King William III, but the original idea was not for Parliament to reign supreme but for sovereignty to be in what is called the *King in Parliament*, in which it is shared between the monarch and the two Houses of Parliament.

Churchill was steeped in what the great Cambridge historian Sir Herbert Butterfield called the *Whig version of history*, and as we saw, this vision, of slow but steady progress, kept both Churchill and the British people going in 1940, when a very different version of history, the Nazi's murderous, racist, ideological interpretation of it, seemed destined to sweep all before it. Whig history was slow but inexorable progress—to call 1689 a revolution is in that sense misleading, since it was more of a coup, with Churchill's great ancestor playing a key military role, than the blood-soaked revolution in France a hundred years later in 1789.

But by definition the rebels of 1776 felt that King George III had betrayed this vision, usurped the rights of the people who were not mere colonists but citizens—no taxation without representation! And in this scenario the British were not the loving mother country but the oppressors of freeborn Americans.

Today we remember that large swaths of the new country had no rights at all—the black slaves. Not, in fact, until the 1960s were *their* rights enshrined in law, after the presidency of Eisenhower and of Churchill's time in office. It was in Eisenhower's time that the first glimmerings of what we now call civil rights began to appear, with marches and court cases slowly pointing the way to the much bigger movement that would emerge in the 1960s.

But to the American elite of the time, and of the period of this book, the key point was not so much the hypocrisy of the past—what has been described as America's original sin, slavery—but the fact that the United States perceived itself to be a nation on the side of colonial peoples wishing their freedom, and Britain as embodying empire, imperialism, alien rule, and all those things from which the heroes of 1776 had liberated themselves in the eighteenth century. Remember the joke in 1943: Britain's South East Asia Command was nicknamed Saving England's Asian Colonies by the Americans.

Self-perception matters—how the United States saw itself and how English-speaking romantics like Churchill regarded it were two different things. Later British prime ministers, such as Harold Macmillan and Harold Wilson, would understand this, and in 1967 Britain began the withdrawal of its vast defense panoply east of Suez, the relics of an imperial age now departed.

Churchill and Eisenhower therefore understood the world in radically different ways. This is where Britain's version of the culture wars have inevitably begun to shape the divergent appreciations of Churchill in two ways, both between those of the United States of America and the United Kingdom, and now too in his own country, as Britons now disagree among themselves concerning his legacy.

As so often, we therefore inevitably return to Churchill's three circles: the United Kingdom *and its empire*, the United States, and Europe. Already by this time, even the first circle was changing drastically. The Dominions—Australia, New Zealand, and Canada—were increasingly looking directly to the United States in their own right as free countries rather than as subsets of the British Empire. India, the former Jewel in the Crown, the Raj of Churchill's youth on the North-West Frontier, had become independent in 1947 and in the Bandung Conference of 1954 had created the Non-Aligned Movement, neither in the capitalist West nor in the Communist bloc. South Africa, a Dominion since 1905, was soon to be expelled from the Commonwealth because of apartheid, not to be readmitted until Nelson Mandela and genuine freedom decades later.

Churchill's conception of a united first circle was in that sense already history. The British Commonwealth still very much exists, with the Queen as its head and embodiment, but nothing like in the sense in which he understood the term—apart from Gibraltar and a few tiny islands, the British *Empire* of which he was so proud has long since departed.

That leaves Churchill's other two circles—the United States and Europe. This is where Britain's twenty-first-century culture wars and the iconic status of Churchill in much of today's America truly determine the perspective in which we see the past—both the "special relationship" of the Second World War and the nature of the United Kingdom's *political* ties to the Europe developing just twenty or so miles across the English Channel while Churchill was still prime minister.

Today there are those who put Britain's relationship with America first, and those who mourn that the close link that the United Kingdom had as a member state of the European Community/Union ended with the "Brexit" referendum in 2016 and formally in 2020. Being Brexit or Remain has become the equivalent of the American culture wars, and sometimes even with the vehemence with which they are being waged in the United States.

But first we must return to history and Churchill's choices in 1940.

In that vital period, from May 1940 to December 1941, this book has consistently argued, Churchill was absolutely right to say that only from America could salvation come. Militarily he was totally correct, and economically as well—to combine these ideas, the United States was indeed the arsenal of democracy. He might have been in a minority to think this—common sense in 1940–1941 was that the Americans would stay isolationist, as Roosevelt himself promised the voters in the 1940 presidential election—but he was completely vindicated. America entered the war and all was changed.

But all was changed in the *West*. The statistic we saw earlier, namely that 85 percent of German casualties were on the *Eastern Front* with the USSR, is one of the most important statistics of the war and alas, in Britain as much as in the United States, completely overlooked. Roosevelt, however, realized that to win the war in Europe, the key power was not Britain but the Soviet Union under Stalin.

Despite many a quarrel and several disagreements, the British and Americans worked superbly as a team from 1941 to 1945, a coalition arguably unique in the history of warfare, and which, on the military and intelligence fronts, has in many ways continued to exist ever since. No two countries have as close a link as the United States and United Kingdom in these two fields including to the present, and in *that* sense the "special relationship," forged by the exigencies of war in 1941, is as operative today as it ever was. During the Second World War the relationship between Eisenhower as Supreme Allied Commander and Winston Churchill embodied the working relationship that won victory in the West.

But one could argue that the "special relationship" *as dreamed by Churchill* was already dead in 1943. Recall once more what happened at Tehran—Churchill humiliated and sidelined by Roosevelt and, by the fact of raw military power, that the Soviets were doing the vast bulk of the fighting against Nazism. Nor was there any partnership of equals on the Western Front. When it came to pass that the United States had far more troops in action in Europe than Britain did, that imbalance, as we saw, became even more pronounced. British troops, along with forces from Canada, Poland, and Free France, all played pivotal roles, but it was the American forces that carried the day.

And if the "special relationship" were not dead in 1943, we have seen that in another sense it was dead by 1953, when Churchill had the pre-inauguration discussions with Eisenhower in New York. On top of those conversations, Churchill refused the American request to join the Vietnam War in 1954, thereby completely derailing the massive anti-Communist coalition that Eisenhower and Dulles wished to put together. This led to the result that we all now know—apart from a contingent of troops from Australia, America was obliged to fight the Viet Minh, with no other outside assistance, until the Communist victory in 1975.

What, therefore, does the "special relationship" mean, if by 1955 it was, *as conceived by Churchill*, already over, even if Churchill himself did not understand that it had ceased to exist in terms of the two circles? Could one argue that in 1941 it succeeded brilliantly and enabled Britain both to be free and on the winning side in 1945, but having done exactly the job for which it was intended, it was redundant and needed no more—except of course in the specialist military and intelligence fields, in which it remains happily alive. And in a real sense, whenever it finished, could it even outlast the person of its founder, Winston Churchill? What, in the 2020s, does the notion of the *English*-speaking peoples possibly still entail?

This is where the third circle—Europe—enters the fray and where the furor now begins! Perspicacious followers of Churchill such as Harold Macmillan had already seen from the late 1940s that *this* was going to be the circle that mattered, down to descendants of Churchill in the 2020s.

Hugo Dixon—the grandson of Churchill's eldest daughter, Diana, wrote in 2019 an open letter to Boris Johnson, soon to be British prime minister and famously the author of a biography of Dixon's great-grandfather, *The Churchill Factor*. As Dixon put it:

> *You love Churchill. You must know one of his favourite poems, The Clattering Train. The last verse goes: For the pace is hot, and the points are near,/ And sleep hath deadened the driver's ear;/ And signals flash through the night in vain./ Death is in charge of the clattering train!*
>
> *You're like that driver on the clattering train, except you're not asleep. Jacob Rees-Mogg and Nigel Farage have persuaded you to sabotage the brakes—and you are hurtling toward the abyss with 66 million people in the back. So some of us are going to have to stop the train for you.*
>
> *Like you, I'm a fighter. But I don't want to fight fire with fire. I prefer to fight fire with water. I prefer Gandhi to Machiavelli. The ends don't justify the means. If we pursue the wrong means, we'll corrupt the ends. Democracy so easily descends into demagogy, as the ancient Greeks knew so well.*
>
> *It's great to be ambitious. But as you stand on the verge of Downing Street, I ask you to reflect. What do you want power for? Surely, it's to fix the country's real problems such as lack of investment in large parts of the country, care for our ageing population and knife crime. Isn't it also to use our influence in the world to fix global problems such as the climate crisis?*
>
> *And can't you see that we'll be much more able to do these things if we stay in the EU? We'll have more money, more power and our*

politicians won't be obsessing about the fallout from Brexit for years.
We have to put the bawling Brexit baby to bed.
   It is not too late to change course. But I'm not counting on that.
You'll probably try to rip us out of the EU without a deal and, when
MPs stop you, call a referendum or an election. At that point, pro-
Europeans have to win the argument. So much is at stake. That's why
I will be going to the grassroots demo in Parliament Square on Satur-
day and saying: "No to Boris, yes to Europe."

So we have a descendant of Churchill employing both Gandhi as
a role model and defending warmly *political* links between the United
Kingdom and what is now the European Union! To many people in Britain, Hugo Dixon is entirely right and Boris Johnson, although the most
devoted Churchill biographer, sadly deluded.

Your author has deliberately used a Churchill descendant, a great-
grandson, for a purpose. For people who believe in Churchill not so much
as a flesh-and-blood person but as an icon, such views are potentially
blasphemous! "Winnie," as he is sometimes described by Eurosceptics
who never knew him in real life, is a political creation of their own making. He has become not someone who existed in real life but a football for
contemporary twenty-first-century political ends.

This is why that to doubt Churchill's infallibility *even in the United*
States is a dangerous thing to do, since he is an emblem for a particular
way of acting, rather than a statesman who had to make hard decisions in
real life, as all politicians of any stripe have to do. The reality of a genuine
Winston Churchill—who refused to join in fighting in Vietnam because
he knew the cataclysmic dangers to Britain of a Soviet nuclear attack as
the result of the United States triggering World War III—is the truth,
but it is not the Churchill that is hero-worshipped in the United States
today.

In fact his refusal is in his defense! It actually shows his wisdom! And
since twenty years after his refusal the Americans actually lost the war in
Vietnam, it shows his foresight and perspicacity as well.

But whether or not he was equally far-sighted in ignoring Europe
depends very much on one's perspective on the internal British and

Continental politics of the twenty-teens and 2020s. To use the title of one of Churchill's books on the Second World War, is Brexit a *triumph* or a *tragedy*? If anyone could have taken Britain into the new European arrangements back in the 1950s, it was Churchill. He was the great moral leader of Europe, even if, in relationship to the United States, as the Eisenhower-Churchill New York talks have revealed, that was no longer the case for the Americans.

There was no possible way in which the United Kingdom, in 1953, could have been even remotely the equal of the United States—militarily, economically, geopolitically, or indeed in any sense at all. But in Europe, Churchill could, if he had so wished, been *primus inter pares*, and under him Britain could have had the leadership of the new Europe for the asking.

When it came to NATO, Britain was, to use Dean Acheson's phrase, present at the creation. But with the nascent European Community, that was not remotely the case, and by leaving the decision to join until after 1958, when the bitter Anglophobic, anti-American Charles de Gaulle assumed power in France, the membership for which thoughtful states-men such as Macmillan longed was postponed until 1973, by which time Europe had evolved on its own without any British input into its formation.

Pro-Europeans have, over the years, blamed Anthony Eden for send-ing a junior Board of Trade official, as an observer not a participant, to the Messina Conference in June 1955, which in turn led to the formation of the European Economic Community in 1957. In one sense this is cor-rect—he was by then prime minister. But what if Churchill had champi-oned Europe when *he* was prime minister from 1951 to 1955? There were certainly plenty in the government who would have supported him—Macmillan was not alone in seeing where the future lay. And Churchill was *Churchill*, the man who saved not just his country but the very free-dom of Western Europe itself in 1940 when he defied Hitler. If anyone could have done it, it was Churchill.

But this did not happen—even though it was a policy for which he would have had the enthusiastic support and blessing of Eisenhower, if he had so chosen. This is one of the great ironies of those who in the 2020s are both pro-American and anti-European: To great statesmen such as Eisenhower, Britain did not have to make the choice—*either* Europe *or* the United States (which is how it is often presented even today) but *pro-*Europe because of being *pro*–United States. It is not, therefore, either/or but both/and: pro-European *and* pro-American, what in American business parlance can be described as a *win–win* outcome.

15

Never Despair

On February 5, 1955, Churchill addressed assembled Commonwealth dignitaries in London for one of their gatherings. In the audience was Lester Pearson, Canadian diplomat and politician and a future winner of the Nobel Prize for Peace. His diary records the gist of what Churchill told the delegates, and it encapsulates, too, the essential difference between the American and British approaches to nuclear weapons, as well as giving a justification for why the United Kingdom now needed such a deterrent of its own. His portrayal of a prime minister in the swansong period of his career is surely accurate.

Churchill really lets himself go on the H-bomb—the shattering implications of which, on society, he has fully grasped. His sweeping imagination and range of mind has sensed that this discovery has made all the old concepts of strategy and defense as out of date as the spear or the Macedonian phalanx. He is horrified and comforted at the same time by the immensity of the bomb, and by its value as a deterrent against Russia. He finds solace in the fact that the Moscow men are cold-blooded realists who know what that power means and don't wish to be destroyed either. So he thinks the bomb may mean the destruction of war, not of humanity.

Churchill quoted, from his recent Cabinet paper on the British deterrent, the wonderful phrase: the "ironic fact . . . we have reached a stage where safety might well be the child of terror and life the twin of annihilation," which he was to repeat in his magnificent address to the House of Commons a few weeks later. Never has the case for deterrence been better put and Churchill's powers of oratory better employed; feeble and frail he might well have been, but his ability to persuade was surely with him until the very end.

Churchill's last speeches as prime minister were on March 14 and 28, 1955, the very last, appropriately, on a memorial for his great First World War predecessor and mentor, David Lloyd George. But the speech that everyone recalls was made on March 1, on the issue of defense, with his closing words "never flinch, never weary, never despair" becoming iconic, and his words echoing down the generations as a rallying call in whatever troubled times we find ourselves, as true now as then.

As he put it at the beginning, the "whole world is divided intellectually and to a large extent geographically between the creeds of Communist discipline and individual freedom." Not only that, he continued, but a situation in which "both sides" possessed "the obliterating weapons of the nuclear age." And ever the historian, he reminded listeners that unlike the Thirty Years War or Mongol times, now we "have force and science, hitherto the servants of man, now threatening to become his master." Churchill understood the issues very clearly indeed.

In fact, as he recalled, following the sage scientific advice of his friend Lord Cherwell, he had predicted the power of nuclear energy in an article he had written twenty-four years earlier, in 1931.

Now three countries possessed such weapons—the United States, the United Kingdom, and the USSR. And the new hydrogen bomb was of an altogether different level of magnitude, where "the entire foundation of human affairs was revolutionized and mankind placed in a situation both measureless and laden with doom."

This was apocalyptic talk! And in another sentence to become famous, Churchill, thinking of young children playing happily, wondered "what would lie before them if God wearied of mankind." (While Churchill was not religious in any theological or other sense of the term, the idea that he might be judged by providence weighed heavily on his mind as he contemplated the nuclear issue and the prospect of mass annihilation that it brought. The historian Kevin Ruane in particular has reiterated this point, and he certainly makes a compelling argument for his case.)

Churchill realized, unlike those both at the time, such as Nobel Prize winner and philosopher Bertrand Russell, and within three years the Campaign for Nuclear Disarmament, that unilateral disarmament was, in reality, not an option. He realized, as we saw earlier, that paradoxically the very threat of mutually assured destruction (MAD) was in fact likely to make such an exchange *less* likely.

This is still a controversial point with pacifists who believe that total unilateral disarmament is the only moral course to follow, which is an entirely acceptable ethical stand to take, both back in the 1950s when many came to believe it, and now in the 2020s when the instability of our global situation has led many to come to the same view. But as Churchill reminded the House of Commons on that epic day, "[S]entiment must not cloud our vision. . . . Facts are stubborn things." If the West disarmed, the Soviets would not.

Indeed, as many have argued since, deterrents actually worked—the nuclear annihilation of *Dr Strangelove* or *On The Beach* never happened, something we know now, looking back from the 2020s, but not possible to predict back in 1955. As he pointed out, there was "widespread belief throughout the world that, but for American nuclear superiority, Europe would already have been reduced to satellite status and the Iron Curtain would have reached the Atlantic and the Channel." Disarmament and deterrence could not be uncoupled.

But where he now went was beyond just the American nuclear shield. *Britain had to have its own nuclear force*: "To make our contribution to the deterrent we must ourselves possess the most up-to-date nuclear weapons, and the means of delivering them." This was not only "a matter of principle," but there were also "many practical reasons," such as the ability of both American and British forces to work immediately together in the event of a Soviet attack on the United Kingdom.

Although Churchill was arguing for an independent British deterrent, he was also very much in tune with American thinking—Eisenhower's New Look—and the need to reduce conventional forces. This was in essence using nuclear weapons to save money, since a defense program that still had to pay for vast land armies was becoming cripplingly expensive, even for a power as major as the United States. But when it came to the Soviet Union, their conventional superiority was taken as a given by both Britain and the Americans.

Churchill was very aware of the "panic" instilled in the public mind by the threat not just of the new weapons themselves but also of the effects of "fall out." But as before he put his faith in deterrence and in the horror of MAD. As he put it, "[A] curious paradox has emerged. . . . After a certain point has been passed it may be said, 'The worse things get the better.'" If the Soviet Union were as vulnerable to nuclear attack as Western Europe, they too would be in "mortal danger."

And then came another famous paragraph:

Then it may well be said that we shall by a process of sublime irony have reached a stage in this story where safety will be the sturdy child of terror and survival the twin brother of annihilation.

Decades after he uttered those words, they have remained true. Perhaps never before or since has the case for deterrence been better made. And subsequent history has vindicated him completely.

(He did allow that "lunatics or dictators" like Hitler in the bunker could be exceptions—this was the main fear during the presidency of Iran of Ahmadinejad, that a rogue ruler could trigger nuclear Armageddon. It is why political analysts refer to "rational actors" and "irrational actors." But as he added, "[W]e may find methods of protecting ourselves, if we are all agreed, against that," and so subsequent history has proved. Whatever their faults, the Soviet Politburo remained rational actors to the end.)

In the rest of his speech, he reiterated the power and effectiveness of deterrence and the need for NATO to stand firm. He ended his oration by emphasizing the need for Britain's *own* nuclear capability, explicitly *not* relying solely on the American nuclear umbrella. This was to become a British mantra over the decades ahead—for the United Kingdom to be able to have its own seat at the table, it had to be a full possessor of its own nuclear arsenal.

As he put it, when it came to relying solely on the United States for protection, as he knew some had argued:

Personally, I cannot feel that we should have much influence over their policy or actions, wise or unwise, while we are largely dependent, as we are today, upon their protection. We, too, must possess substantial deterrent power of our own. We must also never allow, above all, I hold, the growing sense of unity and brotherhood between the United Kingdom and the United States and throughout the English-speaking world to be injured or retarded. Its maintenance, its stimulation and its fortifying is one of the first duties of every person who wishes to see peace in the world and wishes to see the survival of this country.

He ended on a legendary note, one that has never been forgotten, and was, although not his final speech to the Commons, one that showed his ability to make great oratory was with him to the last:

> *To conclude, mercifully, there is time and hope if we combine patience and courage. All deterrents will improve and gain authority during the next ten years. By that time, the deterrent may well reach its acme and reap its final reward. The day may dawn when fair play, love for one's fellow men, respect for justice and freedom, will enable tormented generations to march forth serene and triumphant from the hideous epoch in which we have to dwell. Meanwhile, never flinch, never weary, never despair.*

Churchill never had his great summit. Sadly for him, one did take place, in 1955 and at Geneva. But while there was much talk of "the spirit of Geneva" (to use Eisenhower's phrase), nothing substantive came from it. Of far more importance were two events that happened shortly after his retirement. One was the recognition of the German Federal Republic's independence by the Western Allies and its admission into NATO. The second was the Austrian State Treaty that saw the Soviets withdraw from both their zone of Austria and of Vienna, one of the very few retreats by the USSR. Austria had to remain neutral (like Finland it could not join NATO), but it became unquestionably part of the West. Not until 1989 did freedom come to the German Democratic Republic, with the reunification of Germany taking place in 1990.

But can one say that Churchill failed? The answer is perhaps that if he did, he was heroically unsuccessful. The writer John Young, in his *Winston's Last Campaign*, is surely correct when he writes that Churchill's persistence "was a refreshing departure from the arid tensions of the Cold War." As he concludes:

> *Greatness may be found in imposing failure as well as towering success, and if his search for a Summit may be counted as a failure, it does not necessarily detract from his reputation as one of the greatest twentieth-century statesmen. Willful denigration of Churchill is as*

unhistorical as lauding him as a Superman. He was in the last analysis only a human being, yet even in his dotage, fighting his own decay, an extraordinary one.

To which one can only say amen!

16

Your Old Friend

Ten years after his retirement, Churchill himself was no more. The era of Khrushchev in the Soviet Union was over too, and the Cold War would become more frozen still. Not until 1989 would the peoples of Central Europe be free from the Soviet yoke, over thirty-four years after Churchill uttered these hopeful and prophetic words. And now, more than thirty years after the fall of the Berlin Wall, uncertainty has returned to that part of the world, with self-professed "illiberal democracies" in a country such as Hungary and actual war in Ukraine. The era of fair play and justice for which millions longed in 1989 has for some vanished. The specter of war has returned to Europe, and once again much of our world is not a safe place.

But nuclear war has not happened . . .

Wars in Europe have taken place—most especially in the 1990s in the former Yugoslavia, where we saw fighting and horror of a kind not seen since the Second World War. Even concentration camps returned, such as at Omarska, and the mass slaughter of civilians, such as at Srebrenica. But these were wars between countries without nuclear weapons. And without MAD to deter them, conflicts took place and thousands died. Even in Ukraine, the Russians pretended their forces were not in fact present—when of course they were—and so the non-nuclear analogy holds. Churchill was right: *deterrence deters.*

Britain's very expensive possession of its own nuclear strike force remains controversial in the United Kingdom even today—if by the time you read this Scotland is once again an independent country, it might ask for all the nuclear submarine bases on its territory to be transferred to England. During the presidency of Ronald Reagan, thousands of people in nations such as Britain and Germany convinced themselves that the kind of rogue ruler capable of being an irrational actor was in the White House, and that Armageddon could be around the corner.

The irony is that the talks in 1986 in Reykjavík (with a treaty following in 1987) actually made the world a safer place, a fact alas lost on the quintessentially English and often genteel, upper-class anti-nuclear protestors of Greenham Common, for whom the presence on British soil of such weapons was immoral. But while the days of activism are now mainly in the past, the issue has not gone away.

As I write this, the pro-NATO, pro-treaty Joe Biden has been elected president of the United States. The domestic twenty-first-century internal politics of the United States should rightly be beyond the purview of a book such as this. But as Britain and France discovered during the Trump presidency, the fact that there were still British and French nuclear submarines meant that the situation for those two countries was not as dire as the existential threat posed to nations with borders with Russia had the United States withdrawn the nuclear umbrella or left NATO—the cancellation of treaties signed by no less than Ronald Reagan, the arch-conservative, was not lost on many in Central Europe, whose post-1989/1991 freedoms were now looking dangerously frail.

This is why the idea put forward by Kevin Ruane in his book *Churchill and the Bomb* is so convincing, even if one of the reasons is one he could not have foreseen in 2016 when the book was published.

> *Churchill's decision to build a British H-bomb in June 1954 was, at its most basic level, an expression of dual-containment. The H-bomb would add to the West's overall deterrent vis-à-vis the USSR and thus boost UK security, but just as importantly it would, as he believed, provide Britain with a greater right to counsel restraint in Washington. And as long as nuclear arms stayed sheathed, and as long as the Cold War remained the Cold War, the chance for détente lived on. . . . Accordingly . . . instead of seeking to meet the heightened Soviet threat by backing the Americans come what may in building more and bigger weapons of mass destruction, Churchill, the original Cold Warrior and atomic diplomatist, opted to call time on the Cold War.*

And as Ruane points out, this puts Churchill in an unexpected and highly favorable light. His wish for détente and peace "confirms . . . his capacity to adapt and learn and shows that even in old age he was capable on this most vital of subjects of new and visionary thinking."

A telegram Churchill wrote to Eisenhower on March 18, 1955, on the unfortunate leak and publication of the Yalta papers included the lines: "I am sorry we shall never meet in a Top Level confrontation of our would-be friends, but I hope indeed this applies to political occasions only." A reunion of friends was implicitly always most welcome.

Churchill was hinting at his impending retirement, and this brought out "an acute case of nostalgia" on the part of the president. It evoked, he told the soon-to-retire prime minister, memories of their first meeting in Washington, DC, in December 1941. It is a symbolic letter, since at that time Eisenhower was just an American staff officer and Winston Churchill the prime minister of a still-great country. The United States was still "shuddering from the shock of Pearl Harbor," and in 1942 Britain had the "bitter reality of the Tobruk disaster," news that came when Churchill was in the United States.

Eisenhower recalled:

Somewhere along about that time [1942] must have marked the low point in Allied war fortunes. Yet I still remember with great admiration the fact that never once did you quail at the grim prospect ahead of us; never did I hear you utter a discouraged word nor a doubt as to the final and certain outcome.

Eisenhower was, of course, right in his sentiment. This, as he had correctly gauged, was Churchill's greatest strength—defiance of Hitler against all odds and a sure faith in the ultimate victory that would come. It is why he was right and the naysayers such as Halifax so catastrophically wrong. Churchill's faith in the Great Democracy, the United States, never let him down.

Now Churchill was about to retire—to hand over the premiership, disastrously as it turned out, to Anthony Eden. Eisenhower, though, wished to continue the friendship with his old wartime friend. But the ideology of the Cold War can be seen in what he wrote next. Ever since he had returned to Europe in January 1951 to command NATO forces, he had "valued beyond calculation my opportunities to meet with you, especially when those meetings were concerned with the military and diplomatic problems of the free world and our struggle against the evil conspiracy centering in the Kremlin." (Ronald Reagan was not the first American president to describe the Soviet Union as an evil empire!)

Much of the letter then moved to contemporary issues—including the defense of Taiwan, a matter that has continued to arise even in the twenty-first century. And in the president's desire to get involved in Southeast Asia, in order to "halt Communism dead in its tracks," we see the future American debacle in Vietnam, a theme to which he returned in a letter to Churchill a week later, on March 29, in which he made clear his view that to stand up to Communism in 1955 was vital because of the way in which the democracies had failed to halt Hitler, Mussolini, and Japan in the 1930s.

But there was time for the personal, too. As Eisenhower put it:

> *Because I do so value this long association and friendship with you, I echo your hope that the impending divergence of our lives will apply to political occasions only. Indeed, I entertain the further hope that with greater leisure, you will more often find it possible to visit us in this country—after all, we do have a fifty percent share in your bloodlines, if not in your political allegiance.*

Back in 1940 appeasers such as RA Butler had dismissed Churchill as a half-American adventurer. Now his mother's legacy was a positive asset, and rightly recognized as such.

Eisenhower recognized, in his March 29 epistle, that on the new American policy of resisting Communism in Taiwan and Southeast Asia, he and Churchill differed. But now that the great man was about to retire, he could admit this amicably:

> *You and I have been through many things where our judgments have not always been as one, but, at least on my part, my admiration and affection for you were never lessened. In this long experience, my hope is rooted that the two of us achieve a personal concord that could, in turn, help our two governments act more effectively against Communists everywhere.*

This was a Cold War perspective. But it had been true since 1941 and the disagreements between Britain and the United States on when to invade Europe, in which Eisenhower had been an observer but one—because he had drafted the American plan—in which he was a player.

Churchill drafted a reply to the president's two letters, but the Churchill Papers note that he did not send it. After explaining the domestic British political exigencies of why he was retiring, he concluded with an affirmation of his deeply held beliefs:

To resign is not to retire, and I am by no means sure that other opportunities may not come upon me to serve and influence those causes for which we have both of us worked so long. Of these the first is Anglo-American brotherhood, and the second is the arrest of the Communist menace. They are, I believe, identical.

This was his last missive to Eisenhower as prime minister. Churchill believed in the Anglo-American "special relationship" to the end of his political career—to him it was indeed "the first . . ."

That bedrock on which Churchill put such store would be tested, however, by his successor Anthony Eden. At the farewell dinner on April 4 for Churchill at 10 Downing Street, attended in a very rare act of royal prerogative by no less than the Queen herself and the Duke of Edinburgh, Eden and his wife, in the words of Churchill's outgoing private secretary Jock Colville, literally "jumped the queue" to get ahead of the other guests. Lady Eden (who was also Churchill's niece) had her train torn as a result of the kerfuffle, with the Duke of Edinburgh announcing loudly, "That's torn it, in every sense."

Colville's final recollections of that night have entered British folklore. The guests had left, and Colville was very aware of the fact that this was a historic occasion.

I went up with him to his bedroom, and he sat down on his bed resplendent in his [Order of the] Garter and his Order of Merit, his knee breeches, and he stared at the window and said nothing and I also said nothing thinking that this was his last night after so many years at 10 Downing Street, and perhaps pondering all else that had happened in that room. However his mind was in fact on something else, because after about a minute, he suddenly fixed me with a stern glare and said: "I don't think that Anthony can do it."

In January 1957 Eden resigned as prime minister, his political career and reputation in tatters. Churchill had been right—Eden had failed to do it.

Churchill was not to be as involved in politics as he had thought when he retired—his health and the frequency of strokes saw to that, including a thankfully mild stroke in June 1955. But when consulted by the Queen as to who should succeed the fallen Eden, the great man's preference for Harold Macmillan, the passionate opponent of appeasement in the 1930s, over RA Butler, the enthusiastic supporter of such a policy, played a crucial role in Macmillan's appointment as prime minister. Macmillan, like Churchill, was also half-American and, as we have seen, knew Eisenhower well since their time together in North Africa in the 1940s.

Here, though, we come to British domestic politics and the United Kingdom's own culture wars.

In the United States the main catastrophe created by Eden was the invasion of the Suez Canal, in secret and indeed almost certainly illegal collusion with France and Israel in 1956. The whole policy was based on lies, since the official reason Britain and France gave to seize the Suez Canal was to separate Egyptian and Israeli forces. But the United Kingdom and the French had agreed on Israel's invasion in advance—the whole thing was a sham. Not only that, but it was done without the permission of the United States, and carried out just before the presidential election in November.

Not surprisingly Eisenhower was incandescent, and ordered financial pressure put on Britain forthwith. This had the desired effect, as wiser people such as Harold Macmillan, the chancellor of the exchequer, realized that the United Kingdom would have to withdraw even though, as in Macmillan's case, they had originally favored British military action. France and Britain duly caved in, and Eden, after recuperating in the Caribbean, returned to the United Kingdom and resigned.

Churchill, as a lifelong Zionist, naturally had strong sympathies with Israel, which played a major part in his support of armed intervention. But he naturally realized the hideous damage that Eden's duplicity and action had done to Anglo-American relations.

No longer in office but still in public life as a member of Parliament, he wrote to Eisenhower on November 23, as the consequences of the debacle were unraveling. Despite the recent events in Egypt, he told the president, "I do believe, with unfaltering conviction, that the theme of the Anglo-American alliance is more important today than at any time since the war." For the United States and United Kingdom to fall out over the mess, regardless of rights and wrongs, "would be an act of folly, on which our whole civilization might founder." As he correctly guessed, the USSR would do all it could to benefit from the situation, so much so that the "very survival of all we believe may depend on setting our minds to forestalling them."

He concluded:

I write this letter because I know where your heart lies. You are now the only person who can so influence events both in the UNO [United Nations] and the free world to ensure that the great essentials are not lost in bickering and pettiness among the nations. Yours is indeed a heavy responsibility and there is no greater believer in your capacity to bear it or true well wisher in your task than your old friend.

Here we see the culture war that has bedeviled British politics ever since and, in the 2020s as this is written, does so still. Was Britain a European country? Was it part of the English-speaking world? Or was it, as it was able to be between 1973 and 2019, in a position to be both?

Conclusion

THIS BOOK HAS EXAMINED TWO ASPECTS OF HISTORY.

One of them is the "special relationship" through the prism of two men at the heart of US/UK relations from 1942 to 1955, Winston Churchill and Dwight Eisenhower, and how the balance of power between the two people changed dramatically over a thirteen-year period, a circumstance that would have been utterly impossible to forecast when they first met properly in London in July 1942. The contrast makes the point vividly, with the once mighty British Empire in decline and the hitherto isolationist United States becoming the global hegemon and leader of the free world in place of Britain.

Second, this transatlantic change of balance also helped create the modern world, with results that are arguably still with us, despite Britain's exit from the European Union and America's period of ideological neo-isolationism under Donald Trump.

Let us look first at how the "special relationship" unfolded after Churchill's retirement from power in 1955.

During the mid-1980s various gatherings of the great and the good occurred at the Anglo-American meeting place of Ditchley Park, a place familiar to Churchill thanks to his visits there during the Second World War.

Their thoughts on the "special relationship" were summarized by the doyen of British military historians, Sir Michael Howard, a decorated officer during the war, an official historian who wrote several of the volumes commissioned by the Cabinet Office to describe it, and later a professor not only at Oxford University but also at Yale and one of the founders of the International Institute of Strategic Studies, an institution with bases both in London and in Washington, DC. If he thought something, it was probably true . . .

In describing the thoughts of those assembled to discuss the topic, he summarized:

It would not be too much to say that the "Special Relationship" was the creation of Winston Churchill, and if it survives at all in the United

States it is because of his memory. Churchill was indeed its embodiment. Genetically he was as much American as British, and throughout his long life he saw the two nations as artificially severed halves of a single community which he worked—not only as a statesman but as an historian and a publicist—to reunite.

As Howard reminds us, it was as much this concept as anything else that caused Churchill in the Second World War to know it was the United States that Britain needed to be able even to survive. In this, as we saw, Churchill was unique in this perspective, as trust in the United States was not something shared by many of the British establishment back in the dark days of 1940. Yet come 1941 Churchill was vindicated. With American entry into the war, the United Kingdom was safe—as he had predicted.

But, if it is possible, even someone as great as Sir Michael Howard is not infallible. He puts the finest hour of the relationship in 1943, when Roosevelt and Churchill between them decided the destinies of the world. However, if one considers what happened at the Tehran Conference that year, it was, if anything, Churchill's sad realization that, compared to the behemoths of the United States and USSR, Britain was only a minor player. As someone who believed passionately in his country's empire and its place by right at the top table, that was indeed a bitter pill to swallow.

Sir Michael is surely correct, though, when he goes on to consider the post-war existence of the "special relationship." Neither Clement Attlee in Britain nor Harry Truman in the United States was especially close, and as Sir Michael regretfully notes, "Churchill's attempt to restore the relationship with Eisenhower when he returned to office was humiliatingly rebuffed, and Eden's attempt to take it for granted in 1956 was catastrophic."

Indeed, if we look back at Eisenhower's diary entries for 1953, it is clear that a truly "special relationship" between the United Kingdom and the United States was *already* over by that date—if in fact it had not died a long time before, maybe even as long ago as 1943 at Tehran, when Roosevelt wooed Stalin at the expense of Churchill.

Unfortunately, for any historian looking back at this time from the vantage point of the 2020s, it is all but impossible to avoid political controversy. In the United Kingdom it is inexorably involved in Britain's culture wars, which have for the past few decades torn the country apart over the very core of its national identity, and as of this writing possibly threaten the long-term existence of the United Kingdom as a single entity altogether, if Scotland secedes and if the logic of the European Single Market persuades enough Protestants in Northern Ireland to forego ancient enmities and bring about the reunification of the island of Ireland.

Sir Michael spoke of the relationship acting on three levels: that of the state itself; that of the functioning part, such as the very close military and intelligence links that have existed continuously since 1941; and that of the cultural affinity, something that Churchill the half-American historian recognized as an integral part of the link.

(The one place where the English-speaking world of Churchill's dreams truly still exists is in the sharing of secret intelligence—the *Five Eyes*. This unites Britain, the United States, Canada, Australia, and New Zealand at the deepest sharing of secrets, with other nations such as Germany having friendly status. This has existed, initially with just Britain and the United States, since the war, and is a continuing legacy, still potent in our own times, of the strength of the relationships forged in the struggle against Nazism.)

But looking at a wider perspective, at the governmental and cultural levels, how much of all this is purely one-sided—desperate supplication on the British side and benign indifference, though never hostility, on the American?

Historians reckon that much depends on the individual relationship of president to prime minister—and of course the continuing popularity of and warmth to the Queen, whose reign has been the longest in over a thousand years of English and then British history.

We can see clearly from Eisenhower himself that although he admired, liked, and revered Churchill as an individual, and recognized the man's true and innate greatness, nonetheless in the new circumstances of the early 1950s, the place that Churchill felt Britain inhabited and the realities of geopolitics were two very different things. The United Kingdom and United States were countries that had much in common. But Churchill, and his nostalgia for empire, represented a past that had long since vanished. Nations such as France and soon Germany would be equally important, and therefore the idea of a unique place for Britain was already outmoded. The relationship between the two countries was still special, but not remotely in the unique sense of Churchill's imagination.

And Eisenhower's letter of wrath to Churchill in November 1956 over the deception and perfidy of Anthony Eden shows this to be all too true, and there is no response to the president's epistle by Churchill because after all, what could he have said?

Macmillan had his own preexisting relationship with Eisenhower, and historians have referred to his "Indian Summer" good personal working relationship with Kennedy, to whom he had an indirect family tie (Kennedy's sister Kathleen was married during the war to Lady Dorothy Macmillan's nephew Lord Hartington, who was killed in 1944).

Although Harold Wilson as a Labour prime minister was politically close to Lyndon Johnson, a Democrat president, there was no "special relationship" between the two men, since Wilson, perhaps wisely in retrospect, refused to send British troops to fight alongside the Americans in Vietnam, something Johnson found hard to forgive. Ted Heath, a Conservative prime minister, was strongly pro-European, so saw no need for the old transatlantic ties.

It was under the zealously conservative Margaret Thatcher and her ideological soulmate Ronald Reagan that we really see the "special relationship" blossoming and becoming the kind of bond that Churchill had envisaged. This was one based on firm friendship, passionately held common worldviews, and a working relationship that brought great dividends for both countries. And between Reagan and Thatcher there was genuine mutual respect.

Post-1990 we come closer to treacherous, politically controversial waters, certainly so far as United Kingdom readers would be concerned, because now the issue of Europe raises itself, with all the toxicity that it has created in British politics ever since. It is hard to be objective when such powerfully strong culture war emotions are raised, as has now been the case in Britain for decades.

The 1990s saw the outbreak of civil war in the Conservative Party that in one sense was not resolved until 2019, when the anti-Europeans took effective control of the party to ensure that British exodus from the European Union took place on schedule in 2020. Although the prime minister, Boris Johnson, was a biographer of Winston Churchill, one of the people he expelled from the party, in this case temporarily, was no less than Churchill's deeply pro-European grandson Sir Nicholas Soames, the one descendant of his grandfather to achieve distinction and government office in British politics.

So when it came to German reunification in 1990, President George H. W. Bush was able to support it successfully over the objections not merely of Margaret Thatcher but also of the French president Mitterrand, two national leaders whose wartime memories of the last time that Germany was united ran deep.

The issues in Tony Blair's premiership (1997–2007) are still raw in British politics. Blair had hoped to get Britain back to the heart of Europe but also maintain a close transatlantic relationship. In 2001 his support of the United States after 9/11 gave him heroic status in America that was surely well merited. Both France and Germany equally backed the United States—indeed, the only time that Article 5 of the NATO treaty was implemented was the decision of all the major European members of that alliance to declare that since America had been attacked, they would come to the aid of the United States. British, German, and French troops all fought alongside their American ally in Afghanistan.

But then came the war in Iraq, and Blair's profound wish to ride two horses simultaneously came tragically unstuck. The United States wanted war, while France and Germany did not. It was no longer possible to be both pro-European and pro-American at the same time. He had to choose. And when he told President George W. Bush that the United Kingdom would be behind the United States "whatever," he crossed a Rubicon. The "special relationship" came first, and Britain followed the United States into war in 2003 while France and Germany stood aside.

(Declaration of interest: Your author briefly advised part of the Cabinet Office in 2002—his report is possibly too classified even to read it himself! And he paid one visit to 10 Downing Street in that period, meeting with an official but not with Blair).

His decision to back the United States proved exceedingly controversial in Britain—although he won the 2005 election (a unique third in a row for a Labour prime minister), his glory days were over and he became a highly divisive figure. Not until the election in 2020 of Sir Keir Starmer as leader of the Labour Party—crucially someone who had not been a member of the Blair government—did it become possible for people in that party to admit that their most electorally successful leader in history had any merits at all. His belief in the "special relationship" had cost him his career and his reputation.

Subsequent prime ministers had good working relationships with Washington, but it was not until the conjunction of Boris Johnson in 10 Downing Street in 2019 and President Trump in the White House (after 2016) that the link could be said to be special in any shape or form. And at the time of writing, there is much speculation on how Britain will cope with President Joe Biden. He has longstanding close ties to France and Germany and, of course, as an Irish-American has a "special relationship" of his own with the Republic of Ireland that is bound to influence how he sees the United Kingdom. Johnson prefers the phrase "indestructible relationship," as the word "special" implies "needy," and as the twenty-first century progresses that could be a much more accurate way in which to describe US/UK relations—one that recognizes that the United States is far more powerful but also that the United Kingdom is not some humble suppliant doing its master's bidding. Time will tell!

This is of necessity only a fleeting glimpse at US/UK relations since Churchill retired in 1955 and the damage to that relationship created by the Suez debacle in 1956. As mentioned earlier, one of the major problems of history written *now* is that it reads present-day struggles back into the past. This inevitably distorts how we see both the Second World War and the discussions between Churchill and Eisenhower in 1951 to 1955, as we examine them through the prism of outcomes sixty and more years later, which would have been utterly impossible for the protagonists to have foreseen back *then*.

But one can say that Eisenhower and Churchill, in their different ways, created a new world order that certainly existed down to 1991 and the dissolution of the Soviet Union and the end of the Cold War. Here one can add that they created this as much in their overlapping period of office in the 1950s (1953–1955) as they did by how war ended in 1945. Churchill was no longer the man he used to be in that time, but his understanding of the threats involved in a possible nuclear war show that his grasp of what ultimately mattered was still with him despite his age and infirmities.

As historian John Lewis Gaddis has reminded us, the issue of hindsight has made, for example, the writing of this history of the Cold War very difficult. Now we know it ended in 1989–1991, but no one writing before 1989 ever predicted the extraordinary results that would then occur. And it is only in the hindsight of the 2020s that we also know that many of the lyrical dreams and hopes of 1989 would, in the long term, be tragically unfulfilled.

Inevitably, therefore, the fact that your author writing on the cusp of a Biden presidency makes this a very different kind of book than the one that would have been written had it been possible to keep to the original schedule, with the book released during an existentially different Donald Trump presidency. The message of President Biden in June 2021 was in effect that America is back, and the world order created after 1945 restored, to the enormous relief of many in Europe. But, of course, to write that is to take a strongly Eurocentric viewpoint, and to believe that close US/Europe ties are what a humorous history book written decades ago would describe as a "Good Thing."

But for your author one of the fascinating aspects of writing this book has been the proof events gave to the law of unintended consequences. Decisions made in 1942–1943, as Eisenhower biographer Stephen Ambrose makes so clear, as does Charlemagne Prize–winning historian Timothy Garton Ash, had dramatic down-the-line effects both on how the Western Allies won the war and for the post-war global order that resulted. Where British and American troops found themselves not just in 1945 but also in 1944, both in relation to the Red Army, made a significant difference once the fighting stopped and the wartime alliance morphed into Cold War. This of course meant that Eisenhower, as president in 1953, had to live with the results of decisions made even before he became Supreme Allied Commander in North-West Europe in 1944.

This is not to say that there would have been no Iron Curtain in 1953 had D-Day been in 1943—your author has learned the hard way the dangers of so heretical an opinion! But what it does say, as Ambrose and Garton Ash have helpfully pointed out, that what actually happened—delaying D-Day until June 1944—had massive repercussions that made far more likely a Soviet-dominated Central and Eastern Europe, Communist rule in the nations behind the Iron Curtain until 1989, and, very seriously for world peace, a Berlin in which a small island of Western-ruled zones existed as a hostage to fortune within a Red Army–occupied Communist bloc.

In one sense it was Truman and the group of European statesmen in power after the war that created the new world order that kept the peace. But Churchill's voice remained powerful, his Iron Curtain speech being fulfilled by the creation of NATO in 1949. And its first commander was Eisenhower. So while the two leaders did not create the new geopolitical order in a direct sense, both of them highly influenced what then followed.

There was a major Berlin crisis under Eisenhower, just after the period of our book, in 1958–1959, and then a major escalation in 1961, under Kennedy, which many at the time saw as quite possibly leading to nuclear war and World War III, putting it, arguably, almost if not actually on the same level of threat as the Cuban Missile Crisis not long later. But the world order survived and, more importantly, so did the peace. World War III never happened. Deterrence worked. And in this Churchill's realization of the dangers of mutually assured destruction (MAD) played a key role.

The reality of the 2020s, that the new global behemoth to rival the United States is the People's Republic of China, would have been inconceivable to both Churchill and Eisenhower, and arguably would have been so until well after the fall of the original rival superpower the USSR in 1991. China's rise is a very recent phenomenon indeed.

But in the 1950s it was already making itself felt, in the Korean War and in the much longer struggle for Vietnam. Eisenhower was certainly aware of its potential dangers, and Churchill was not ignorant of them either. The settlement in 1954 that divided Vietnam in two was a diplomatic triumph for Churchill's eventual successor, Anthony Eden, and America had to concede that its hope for a non-Communist Vietnam would not be feasible.

Eisenhower did not involve the United States directly in the Vietnam War, but even the limited role that the United States played unwittingly left a legacy for his successors, which was eventually to result in American defeat and the whole of Indochina becoming Communist.

Churchill was wise to keep the United Kingdom out of Vietnam— people remember that Harold Wilson defied President Johnson over the issue but forget that Churchill was ever involved in the debate a decade or so earlier.

Eisenhower and American administrations since (with the exception as ever of Trump) strongly supported British involvement in Europe, and particularly in active membership of what became the European Union. (Remember that Dean Acheson specifically rejected Churchill's three circles concept of Britain with the United States, Europe, and the Empire/ Commonwealth.)

Politically this issue remains highly toxic in the United Kingdom to this day—the Brexit debate and decision in 2016 and the narrowness of the result launched the country into a profoundly divisive culture war from which it arguably has not yet emerged, and might not do so for a long while to come. (It could, as we saw, *perhaps* lead to the dissolution of the United Kingdom itself, though that outcome is not necessarily in the near future.)

Eisenhower saw Britain as needing to get closer to Europe. Churchill, for all his wonderfully pro-European rhetoric in the 1940s when he was in opposition, did not. When Eisenhower's wartime colleague in North Africa, Harold Macmillan, became prime minister in 1957 and tried subsequently to take Britain into the newly created European Economic Community, the time for the United Kingdom to take a lead in such an organization—which under Churchill's premiership could have, with his prestige, been Britain's for the taking—had passed and Britain did not join the European Community until 1973.

In 2016 a narrow margin in a referendum caused Brexit, with formal British exit in January 2020. At time of writing the long-term results are by definition unknowable, and as always with this highly charged emotional debate, everything depends on the individual's point of view—British readers of this book will probably be as split as the country itself was back in 2016.

So how costly was Churchill's rejection of Eisenhower's views? Here it is possible that how one reacts depends on one's political views in the United States as well as in Britain. Up to and including George W. Bush's presidency—from Eisenhower to the younger Bush if one likes, including under Republicans—the United States wanted Britain *in Europe*, and President Obama in 2016 campaigned overtly for the British to vote to remain. However, as with many issues, candidate Trump publicly supported Leave and continued to do so as president. Today, therefore, while Brexit horrified the American establishment, many an ordinary citizen—presuming that they even thought about Britain, which may be unlikely—might have been cheering the Brexiteers on.

And is the "indestructible relationship," for which Churchill sacrificed closer ties with Europe, worth Britain's exclusion from 1957 to 1973, uneasy membership from 1973 to 2016 and 2020, and formal separation since 2020? If many of Churchill's own descendants are Europhile Remainers—at least those who have publicly entered the debate—who are we to contradict them? Britain, until 2016, was arguably a nation that voted on social class and economics, the Labour Party always having a smattering of Fabian intellectuals to go alongside the often-Methodist Trade Unionists. Now Britain seems to have shifted in the same direction as the United States, with education level being one of the key determinants of how people vote. Nostalgia for the kind of country that Churchill took for granted is more likely among those who never went to university than those who did.

So for Remainers (such as your author, which is surely obvious), Churchill's path not taken was a tragedy, not a blessing. For intellectual Brexiteers (and they do very much exist), such as his most popular biographer Andrew Roberts, the Anglosphere has always been more important, the ties with the United States and the English-speaking majority-European Commonwealth countries (such as Canada, Australia, and New Zealand) far more vital for Britain's role on the global stage than the ties with the Europeans across the Straits of Dover.

This book is about how Churchill and Eisenhower embodied the rise of the "special relationship" and how they created the modern world. In 1939 to 1941 Churchill was surely right beyond peradventure to say that only with American aid could Britain survive and end up on the winning side. Men such as Chamberlain grossly exaggerated British power in a way that Churchill did not. He understood the geopolitical realities. As said more than once in these pages, in December 1941 he was vindicated and in 1945 proved correct.

But of course as his fate at Tehran in 1943 showed, the "special relationship" was distinctly lopsided. Once the invasion of Europe finally began, American military predominance soon showed itself. And by the time that Eisenhower became president, that imbalance became ever more striking. However hard Churchill tried to persuade his old wartime comrade, if the United States had made up its mind, there was nothing that the British prime minister could do.

The Five Eyes intelligence-sharing network is not just part of the "special relationship" but also arguably the Anglosphere in living reality. And in the uncertain times in which we live in the 2020s, it surely shows its ongoing value to our security today, especially with the rise of China to superpower status. NATO too, post-2021, shows it remains relevant, though there Britain shares its links to the United States with a whole host of other countries, from the Atlantic to the Baltic.

So Churchill and Eisenhower helped create the modern world. By Churchill's retirement in 1955, that world had changed immeasurably. In 1956, because the Eden government deliberately kept the United States out of the loop on collusion with France and Israel over the Suez Canal crisis, Eisenhower was able to use raw financial power to compel the United Kingdom to make an ignominious withdrawal from Egypt. Some "special relationship"!

His wartime colleague Harold Macmillan, under one interpretation of what happened next (the one your author follows), when he became prime minister in 1957, restored relations with the United States but at the same time began the process that would, as we saw, lead to the United Kingdom joining the EU in 1973, a direction that both his predecessors, Churchill and then Eden, had rejected, and at a time when Britain could have easily become a key leader of the new Europe, with a European Economic Community reflecting British industrial interests as much as those of French farmers in the Common Agricultural Policy. As we have also seen, the United States, while hewing close to Britain in matters such as Five Eyes and NATO, strongly approved of British membership in what became the EU. In that sense we can say that Eisenhower was right. For not only was Churchill still living in the dream world of empire and British greatness, so too was much of the country: It was not until several major financial crises, for example, that the Labour government of Harold Wilson finally agreed in 1968 to withdraw British forces from "East of Suez" in 1971. The United Kingdom was both in Europe while friends with the United States.

Many devotees of Churchill and the Anglosphere would of course see it differently. They perceive the years 1973 to 2020 as ignominious and the referendum of 2016 resurrecting the Churchillian three circles, albeit in new circumstances. Here again, who is right all depends on your politics. Eisenhower and Macmillan were surely right, though, to say that the British Empire had had its day—Harold Macmillan's "winds of change" blew through not just Africa but much of Asia as well, with nations from Ghana to Malaysia gaining their independence in just a few short years, mainly under Macmillan's premiership. A Britain without an empire would have seemed strange to Churchill, but that is what happened.

Now it is too early to tell what will happen next, and the interpretation of readers will as always differ according to their political outlook. Depending on one's point of view, Britain has either rejected the modern world or rediscovered its identity. Either way the three circles policy beloved by Churchill is back, with Britain reaching out to nations such as Australia for renewed trade ties, maintaining its close relationship with the United States (whatever adjective one uses to describe it), and being near to Europe but not in it.

But now the latest rival hegemon is China, not the USSR, and that is an entirely new set of circumstances that Eisenhower and Churchill could never have foreseen in their lifetimes. They created a whole new world, but post-1991 another kind of new world order arrived with the disintegration of the Soviet Union and the rise of varying degrees of religious nationalism. Thirty years after those historic events, it is hard to assess whether we are in yet another configuration or still dealing with the effects of 1989 to 1991 and the disappearance of the bipolar two-superpower world order of 1945 to 1991. It is, as Zhou En-lai probably did not say about the French Revolution, too soon to tell.

Bibliography

I BEGAN THIS BOOK BEFORE THE COVID-19 LOCKDOWN, WHICH WAS fortunate, but much of the writing was done under lockdown conditions. I therefore was not able to visit the National Archives in Kew, England, in person, or see the Eisenhower Papers in Abilene, Kansas. However, I was rescued, thanks to the wonderful director of the Churchill Archives in Cambridge, England, and by the Churchill Papers put together by the excellent team at Hillsdale College in Michigan. In particular, volume 23 of this series, published in 2019, proved to be a gold mine.

This volume has numerous extracts from the National Archives, especially of the minutes of cabinet meetings in London (CAB 128) and Churchill's prime ministerial papers (PREM 11). In addition much of the Churchill-Eisenhower correspondence quoted in the book is contained in several places: in Churchill Papers (Vol. 23, PREM 11), and also in the file devoted to the correspondence in the Churchill Archives (CHUR 2/217), with some of the letters published in book form.

Churchill's speeches to the House of Commons are also in the Hillsdale College volume. Quotations from Jock Colville's *The Fringes of Power* are taken from the extracts in the same work.

Most of Eisenhower's diaries have been published, but some were omitted from the original published version in 1990; for them I have used those quoted by Professor Kevin Ruane in his book *Churchill and the Bomb*. I also used the material on Eisenhower in the George C. Marshall Papers, held in the library dedicated to Marshall at the Virginia Military Institute, of which I made use many years ago.

As much as possible I used material that is Crown Copyright, use of which is thankfully free. Much of the Eisenhower material used is contained in the PREM 11 files.

In many cases a particular book used was the one in possession of the Roskill Library at Churchill College Cambridge (connected to the Churchill Archives), so that some books are the US edition and some the British, and some the paperback not the hard-cover copy.

Ambrose, Stephen E. *Eisenhower 1890-1952*. New York, NY, 1983.

Ambrose, Stephen E. *The Supreme Commander*. London, 1971.

Ben-Moshe, Tuvia. *Churchill: Strategy and History*. Boulder, CO, 1992.

Boyle, Peter G., ed. *The Churchill-Eisenhower Correspondence 1953-1955*. Chapel Hill, NC, 1990.

Catherwood, Christopher. *Churchill: The Treasures of Winston Churchill, The Greatest Briton*. London, 2012.

Catherwood, Christopher. *His Finest Hour*. London, 2010.

Catherwood, Christopher. *Winston Churchill*. London, 2019.

Catherwood, Christopher. *Winston Churchill: A Reference Guide to His Life and Works*. Lanham, MD, 2020.

Catterall, Peter, ed. *The Macmillan Diaries: The Cabinet Years, 1950-1957*. London, 2003.

Charmley, John. *Churchill's Grand Alliance*. London, 1995.

D'Este, Carlo. *Eisenhower: Allied Supreme Commander*. London, 2004.

Eisenhower, Susan. *How Ike Led*. New York, NY, 2020.

Farmelo, Graham. *Churchill's Bomb*. London, 2013.

Ferrell, Robert H., ed. *The Eisenhower Diaries*. New York, NY, 1981.

Grigg, John. *1943: The Victory That Never Was*. London, 1980.

Hastings, Max. *Finest Years: Churchill as Warlord 1940-45*. London, 2009.

Hitchcock, William L. *The Age of Eisenhower*. New York, NY, 2019.

Holmes, Richard. *In the Footsteps of Churchill*. London, 2005.

Keegan, John. *Winston Churchill*. London, 2002.

Korda, Michael. *Ike: An American Hero*. New York, 2007.

Larres, Klaus. *Churchill's Cold War*. New Haven, CT, 2002.

Louis, Wm. Roger, and Hedley Bull, eds. *The Special Relationship*. Oxford, 1986.

Ramsden, John. *Man of the Century*. London, 2002.

Reynolds, David. *In Command of History*. London, 2004.

Roberts, Andrew. *Churchill: Walking with Destiny*. London, 2018.

Roberts, Andrew. *Masters and Commanders*. London, 2008.

Ruane, Kevin. *Churchill and the Bomb*. London, 2016.

Smith, Jean Edward. *Eisenhower in War and Peace*. New York, NY, 2012.

Young, John. *Winston Churchill's Last Campaign*. Oxford, 1996.

Index